80 DISPATCHES
⇒ *from the* ⇐
DEVIL'S DOMAIN

Randall Tremba

Published by Four Seasons Books
114 W. German Street
Shepherdstown, West Virginia 25443
Phone: 304.876.3486
Website: fourseasonsbooks.com

© 2021 by Randall Tremba

TABLE OF CONTENTS

- v PREFACE
- vii ACKNOWLEDGMENTS
- ix FOREWORD
- 1 BACKSEAT DRIVER
- 3 ELEVEN IS WEIRD
- 5 THROUGH THE EYES OF DARWIN
- 7 FLAMETHROWER
- 9 PUSHING MY LUCK
- 11 SWIMMING WITH THE SHARKS
- 13 OFF THE BEATEN PATH
- 15 KILL ME A SON
- 17 APOCALYPSE
- 19 RITA
- 21 IS MARRIAGE HAZARDOUS?
- 23 JESUS SHAVES
- 25 COWSHIT
- 27 OLD LETTERS
- 29 A NEW DAY AT SPC
- 31 YOGA SAVES!
- 33 DEEP DARKNESS
- 35 IMAGINE NO RELIGION
- 37 JOY IN MUDVILLE
- 39 HOPE FOR OUR COUNTRY
- 41 LOVE IN VEGAS
- 43 MAGICAL MYSTERY TOUR
- 45 BON VOYAGE, DEAR FRIEND
- 47 SYMPATHY FOR THE JOKER (Just in time for the Oscars)
- 49 SAVING JESUS
- 51 LOOKING FOR JESUS
- 53 THE GREENING OF SOUTHERN WEST VIRGINIA
- 55 HILLBILLY HOT DOGS (A Love Story)
- 57 AN ACT OF GOD?
- 59 BIRDS ARE BUDDHISTS
- 61 ZOOM (A love story)
- 63 WORLD WAR III
- 65 EASTER 2020 (I saw Jesus today)
- 67 RESURRECTION (A week later)
- 69 CRUCIFIXION (Lest Easter make us forget!)
- 71 RESURRECTION SEX (Breaking news!)
- 73 TRUST SCIENCE

75 HOW TO STOP A REBELLION	**121** OUR SIDE WON
77 EXPLOSIVE DEVICE	**123** THANKSGIVING
79 RACISM IS SIN	**125** A DAY OF MOURNING
81 FOR MOTHERS (On Father's Day)	**127** A LONG DARK WINTER
83 BORN INNOCENT (What happened?)	**129** NIGHT
	131 VACCINE
85 BORN ON THE 5TH OF JULY	**133** STAR OF BETHLEHEM
87 HAPPINESS	**135** BAPTISM OF JESUS SUNDAY
89 GRAVEN IMAGES	**137** STORMING THE CAPITOL
91 AT THE BEACH	**139** NAPOLEON EXILED
93 ODE TO EVE	**141** WELCOME TO EARTH, BABY
95 ODE TO THE BIKE	**143** SUPER BOWL 2021 (Revisited)
97 FOR SUCH A TIME AS THIS	**147** VALENTINE'S DAY (Ugh!)
99 SYMPATHY FOR THE DEVIL	
101 SHIP OF FOOLS	**149** GIVING UP LENT
103 A LAMENT FOR EVANGELICALS	**151** NOT LONG TO LIVE
105 BEELINE MARCH	**153** WIZENED BEAUTY
107 HOUSE ON FIRE	**155** ARE WE ALONE?
109 STILL WATERS	**157** EARTH IS OUR GIG
111 POSITIVE THINKING	**159** MARY DON'T YOU WEEP
113 MIRACLE ON PATRICK STREET	**162** ABOUT THE AUTHOR
115 THE GOD WHO SMITES	
117 GOODBYE, MR. PRESIDENT	
119 WHAT, ME WORRY?	

PREFACE

For 40 years before I retired in 2017, I wrote a sermon nearly every week and an essay every three months for the Shepherdstown *Good News Paper*. That's 2,000 sermons and more than 100 essays.

People listened to what I said. People read what I wrote. I heard cheers and boos. I was relevant and didn't even know I was relevant until someone asked me soon after my retirement how it felt to be irrelevant.

I wasn't sure whether that was an insult or a joke. But I took that question into my retirement cave. I sat down, sighed, and unwound. After 40 years of being in the arena, I quickly got used to being in a cave. It was bliss.

And then one day, out of the blue, the devil found me.

You know, you used to be somebody. But now you're irrelevant. Looks like you're hiding your light under a bushel. I like that. When you were letting it shine you gave me fits with your relentless chattering and scribbling about peace, love, and understanding. Stupid people fell for that crap, but I wanted to throw up. Such garbage. I hope you rot in this cave and never write a single word again.

The devil left in a huff. But he also left a gift.

I started whistling. *This little light of mine I'm gonna let it shine. Hide it under a bushel? No! Never!* I had forgotten how much I loved that song.

Yes, of course, your light may be small—but it's yours. Who knows how or why that light gets in us? It just does. One day, out of the blue, you see something in yourself you'd not seen before.

So I told the devil: Beware. I'm stepping out. I'm gripping my pencil. I'm getting back in the arena. I will bring prosperity to West Virginia, democracy back to America, and peace to the world.

But first I needed to take a nap.

When I woke up a friend called me and said: *You're not done. You need to keep writing. Why don't you launch a blog and post something every Sunday morning. After all, you used to deliver a sermon every Sunday for 40 years.*

So I did. And of course I named it "The Devil's Gift."

Thanks to Ol' Scratch I post a reflection most Sundays on something I find remarkable in and around my world. This book is a collection of dispatches from the first two years of my blog. You can subscribe to "The Devil's Gift" at www.thedevilsgift.com.

ACKNOWLEDGMENTS

First, I want to thank Bill Howard for coaxing me to start a blog. He created the site, maintains it, and helps me find images for each post. Bill has a keen eye for what's just right. At first, I thought text alone would be enough. Bill didn't. I'm glad he persisted. I now see that images speak in ways that words can't. Many images herein appear courtesy of The Downstream Project, for which Bill is the executive director. (You can see the images in original color on the blog site. www.thedevilsgift.com.)

Next I want to thank Libby Howard for editing each post. On Mondays, I send her a "perfect" draft only to find out it's not perfect. So I amend the first draft, and the second, and the third, and sometimes a fourth and a fifth. I don't know anyone else who does what she does. But I do know no one's better at it. Libby sees things an eagle's eye would miss.

I also want to thank Kendra Goldsborough, proprietor of Four Seasons Books, and Ed Zahniser, Shepherdstown's Poet Laureate, for advising me on the production and publication of this book. Their encouragement kept me going when doubts and challenges arose.

I also want to thank the design team at HBP (Hagerstown, Maryland), especially Lori Schulman and Dawn Winter-Haines, for their enthusiastic support and creative work designing this book.

I also want to thank my wife Paula for providing stunningly beautiful photos to grace my blog's home page. Now and then Tom Taylor lends a hand in composing montages of her photos. Thank you, Tom. (You can browse Paula's photo gallery at www.paulatrembaphotographs.com)

I also want to thank Hoppy Kercheval for giving this book a boost with his gracious and upbeat Foreword.

Finally, I want to thank the 350 plus subscribers to my blog, most of whom read it every Sunday. Their positive responses and apt comments are gifts to me.

Randall Tremba

FOREWORD

by Hoppy Kercheval
Host of MetroNews Talkline
Vice President of West Virginia Radio Corporation

Red Smith, the Pulitzer Prize winning sports journalist, said of his profession, "Writing is easy. All you have to do is sit down at the typewriter, cut open a vein, and bleed."

Writing—really good writing—is incredibly difficult, and yes, even painful.

As a talk show host and columnist, I struggle to write commentaries that are coherent, interesting, accurate, and, once in a great while, even poignant.

Somehow, Randy Tremba has found a way to master the craft.

The title of his book—*80 Dispatches from the Devil's Gift*—suggests he may have cut a deal with Ol' Scratch himself for the gift. (Randy will only admit to an unholy conversation with the devil as his inspiration.)

I am joking, of course. (I think.)

Randy spent four decades flexing his intellectual muscle through weekly sermons, marriage ceremonies, funeral services, and countless conversations with, well, anybody and everybody.

As a result, Randy has become a keen observer of life. The topics of his observations range from weighty issues of justice and peace to what it means to lose your favorite tree. He finds meaning in the mundane as well as the spiritual.

He writes in short sentences that are simple, but powerful. Consider these: "The ash trees in my woods are dying. They don't know what's eating them. They don't know a pest has doomed them. They don't know a chainsaw is coming."

If Randy had written, "The diseased trees on my property are being cut down," I wouldn't care. It's his writing style that has piqued my curiosity about these trees, and I know there will be a deeper lesson in there somewhere.

That is another beauty of *Dispatches*. You can make quick work of an entertaining anecdote, often tinged with self-deprecating humor, or allow the story to settle and seep into your soul for further reflection.

My parents attended Randy's church for many years. He became a dear friend of the family. He officiated my father's funeral. I remember listening to his homily and thinking that he had taken the time to really know my father; as a result his remarks captured the essence of the man.

It was the work of not only a good writer but a good listener. Only a person who pays close attention can convey equally well the meaning of a dying tree and the meaning of a dying loved one.

Good Christians spend their lives trying to avoid the devil. But he is constantly bombarding us with temptation, even while we are sitting in or working for the church.

Randy Tremba thought he was finished with his work. Enough sermons and counseling, no more funerals or weddings. Just a quiet, relaxing retirement filled with family, friends, morning walks and afternoon naps. He would let someone else wage the battle against the devil.

But the devil found Randy again. And as you read *Dispatches*, you will be glad he did.

BACKSEAT DRIVER
June 30, 2019

So, I'm driving my 4-year-old grandson Wyatt home after an all day visit at our house.

He's strapped snugly in his car seat in the back seat. Not much wiggle room. Bulky headrest blocks his view.

Still, he always seems to see the road ahead. A deer crossing. A school bus stopping.

We're listening to "classic rock" on the radio. A squirrel darts in front of the car.

I see it. I do not swerve.

"Did you miss that squirrel, Grandy?"

I don't know.

"But you didn't try, did you?"

No, I didn't. Squirrels zigzag so fast you can't tell where they'll be next. So, it's best to just keep going straight and trust your luck.

"Well, then, maybe you should slow down!"

I turned up the radio.

ELEVEN IS WEIRD
July 21, 2019

So my 10-year-old granddaughter Angie is sitting beside me as we drive back to Shepherdstown from Boonsboro after returning her younger cousins, Eli and Wyatt, back home after nine hours of merry mayhem. I'm feeling relief. Angie is forlorn.

"Grandy, I'm sad," she tells me.

Why are you sad?

"Because I'll be leaving pretty soon."

After a monthlong visit, she and her twin sister, Paula, will return to Albuquerque next week.

That's sad for me, too. But you know what? You'll be starting fifth grade next month. Fifth grade! Imagine that!

"Yeah, I know. I really love school. But then the next month I'll be *11*. And 11 is such a *weird* age."

That startles me.

Hey! Are you making fun of me?

"No, why?"

Because for the past year I've been saying over and over I couldn't wait to be 72. I didn't like being 71 because it felt like being 11. I mean, 11 is like limbo.

I'm not sure Angie knows what limbo is, but she agreed.

"Yep. I don't think I'm gonna like being 11. I really can't wait to be 12."

Which confirms my theory about 11. Nobody wants to be 11. But 12? Everybody likes turning 12. It has a nice ring to it. It's a threshold. It connotes a certain maturity and status. Like 72, I suppose.

So, Angie, why do you want to be 12?

"Because I can do things at 12 that I can't do at 11."

I slow down a little and turn the radio off. I'm thinking.

What does New Mexico allow at age 12? What have her parents told her about being 12? What have her peers told her? And more to the personality of this particular and peculiar granddaughter, what has she *imagined* she can do at 12 that she can't do at 11?!

Angie.

"Yes."

What can you do at 12 that you can't do at 11?

"I can go to the gym with my mom."

I turn the radio back on, speed up a little and think of all the things I can do at 72 that I couldn't do at 71.

THROUGH THE EYES OF DARWIN
August 4, 2019

I left the church two years ago. I thought I was just retiring but now I see I left it in more ways than one. I haven't been back since—to that one or any other.

After 42 years I'm glad I could leave a strong, vigorous, and kind-hearted congregation behind. I'm proud to have had a hand in cultivating a community with a reputation for courage, creativity, and hospitality. I'm grateful to have left behind a "garden" that's growing and thriving.

People ask, "But don't you miss it?"

Yes, I miss the people. I miss the children. I miss my co-workers. I miss the tilling, the weeding, the harvest. I don't miss the God that came with the turf.

A woman tilled and cultivated her garden day after day, year after year. Her pious neighbor noticed how luscious that garden was. One day he called out: "The Lord sure has blessed you with a beautiful garden!" The gardener replied, "Well, you should have seen it when the Lord was tending it on his own!"

The gardener didn't expect God to make the world a better place. The neighbor apparently did. I'm with the gardener. A God that saves some but not others just doesn't make sense to me anymore.

I've left that God behind.

And I'm pretty sure that's the kind of God Jesus left behind in the third temptation. "Jump and God will save you!" said the devilish Trickster. "God will save you! *It says so in the Bible!*" (Yes, the devil quotes the Bible! Often on television!)

No, thank you, replied Jesus. *I don't trust in that kind of God.*

Neither do I.

Darwin left God out of the natural world and saw truths not seen before. I now read the Bible through the eyes of Darwin and leave God out of it. It makes more sense that way. Which is to say: humanism makes more sense to me than theism. But just to be clear: *either without compassion is worthless.*

FLAMETHROWER

August 11, 2019

I read the news today, oh boy. A crazed man killed 22 in El Paso and another killed nine in Dayton. And though that news was very sad, thousands more were killed or left to die that same day in a hundred other places. Those deaths didn't make the news. When you're watching the circus, you miss a lot.

In case you hadn't heard, Cain killed Abel, too. That's not news. And it's not history. It's a mythic folk tale, which means *it never was but always is.*

Cain wasn't a "killer ape." He wasn't a hunter. He grew vegetables. But the world wounded him. Rage smoldered within.

Cain is in all of us.

Cain killed his brother and then went on to build the first city, civilization, you might say. It produced art and technology, music and tools, vaccines and solar panels and, of course, guns.

Humans make things. It's what we do. We're ingenious.

Other animals make things too. Beavers make dams. Bees make hives. Birds make nests. But no other animal can make a gun. Oh, sure, apes swing clubs and chimps fling turd balls, but only humans make flamethrowers.

As George Carlin put it: "The very existence of flamethrowers proves that sometime, somewhere, someone said to themselves, *You know, I want to set those people over there on fire, but I'm just not close enough to get the job done.*"

Someone got the job done.

And now that we see so many places on fire, we need to get another job done. And we can. We're humans. We're ingenious. And devious. We mess up a lot. But if we don't fix it, nobody else will.

And that, by the way, is pretty much Humanism 101. It's one way to see things. But it's not the only way.

PUSHING MY LUCK
August 18, 2019

I don't believe in thoughts and prayers. I don't believe in tarot, Ouija or I Ching. I don't believe in providence, fate, or luck. I don't believe in messiahs, miracles, or silver bullets.

I don't believe in progress. I don't believe things are moving inevitably toward a better world.

I believe in people. I trust people to get things done. I believe in work.

I trust people because I don't know what else to trust. I trust people because people create such amazing things: art, music and poetry, not to mention toilets, prosthetics, vaccines, therapies, disease-resistant crops, bridges, treaties, trade agreements, safe cars, safe planes, and laws to protect the vulnerable from the ruthless.

And yet, people mess up. Sometimes horribly.

We allow famine, war, and global warming. We create flamethrowers, bombs and assault weapons. We allow the powerful to screw the weak and laugh about it up their sleeves.

Still, I trust people to work things out. I'm hopeful.

After all, I don't believe in "original sin." I believe in "original blessing." I believe we have it in us to do great things. I trust people to see what's gone wrong, make it right, mend the world, and keep at it endlessly.

And then I remember Sisyphus.

Sisyphus was condemned by Zeus to push a giant boulder up a steep hill. He never clears the top with it. It always rolls back down to the bottom. Endlessly. It's a myth, of course, which means *it never was but always is.*

Sometimes I worry that I'm Sisyphus and that trusting people is pushing my luck like a giant boulder up a steep hill.

SWIMMING WITH THE SHARKS
August 25, 2019

My young friend is drowning. He can't keep his head above water. Now he's under. Now he's up.

I would toss him a lifeline. But he doesn't want it.

He's not afraid of dying. Been there. Done that, he tells me. Totally flatlined once. No big deal.

He's a bloghead like me. I read his posts. He reads mine. His are sometimes somewhat dark. He tells me not to worry. I worry. I can't help it. I'm afraid death will be a letdown for him.

It's not either-or, he tells me. It's both-and. Dying and living. The same thing.

I'm not smart enough to agree or disagree. I just know that I like it here. Besides, I don't know if there's a *there* anywhere else. I sure wish he could like it *here* more. But I don't know if he can.

I once held him when he was just a newborn. He was a bundle of light. He could have been a star at most anything. But at age three his world was blown up.

Eventually, he hopped on the candy train. It's a train that never stops. Still he manages to get on and off. He's a hopeless dope addict, he tells me. And a hopeless hope addict. Both-and.

He's cursed and blessed. And knows it.

He doesn't believe in original sin. He believes in original suffering. To be human is to suffer, he tells me. Life is hard. It just is.

I think he's drowning. He tells me he's swimming with the sharks.

He knows the story of creation. He knows it begins in darkness and chaos. He knows it's not history. He knows it's a myth—that it never was but always is.

He knows darkness is pregnant with light. He knows life arises out of death time and time again. And he knows knowing is not enough.

I can't tell if my young friend is swimming or sinking. I do know he's sunk to the bottom enough to know darkness as an old friend. He knows the sound of silence.

I don't throw him a lifeline. He already has one.

OFF THE BEATEN PATH
September 1, 2019

My old friend moved away. He didn't want to but he had to, he said. He'd lost the ranch along with a marriage.

He didn't blame it on luck. He didn't blame it on God. He isn't superstitious or religious, though he does like gospel music.

He worked hard to provide for his family. His friends know him as a salt of the earth guy.

We gathered on the eve of his departure. We shared memories. Laughed. Cried. And finally gave him a round of hugs.

He said he'd miss his old familiar haunts. He'd miss all of us. He assured us he'd be fine. Kin had turned up a vacant house for him up some holler on the edge of the world with a whiff of cellular service.

It's true he'd lost a lot. But he still had his vintage pick-up and his shaggy dog. And that was enough, he told us.

A few days after he left, I called to see how he was doing. We spoke of old friends, health, and the weather. He said that where he lived there was no weather. *I live so far off the beaten path weather doesn't come out this far.*

That's a long way from anywhere, I thought. Are you sure you're all right?

Absolutely! I got a roof over my head, food in the fridge, and a rocking chair on the porch. I got my truck and my dog. I'm doing fine. Really!

A month or so later, he took his truck in for its annual inspection. It failed. He put it out to pasture and bought a used car.

Next, his dog got sick. He took it to the vet. He spent every penny he had to give it a chance. It died.

And that, I thought, would kill him for sure.

I saw him a few months later. He looked good and sounded great.

I didn't think you'd survive the loss of your truck and your dog back to back, I told him. How did you?

God helped me, he said.

I guess we're never too far off the beaten path.

Where can I go from your spirit? Or where can I flee from your presence. If I ascend to heaven, you are there; if I make my bed in Sheol, you are there.
Psalm 139

KILL ME A SON
September 8, 2019

A friend asked me to explain what Jesus meant by this: *Unless you hate your father, mother, brothers, sisters, wife and children, and, yes, even life itself you cannot be my disciple.* (Luke 14:26)

I told my friend: *It means I can't be his disciple. I can't meet that requirement even if "hate" in the original Greek text means "disregard" rather than "disdain."*

I imagine myself saying to Jesus, *Sorry, but I can't do that*. And I imagine Jesus saying, *That's OK, brother. This path is not for everyone. Stay home with your family and be good to them. Nothing wrong with that.*

Look, I told my friend, being a Christian is easy. Following Jesus is hard. I'm not about to sacrifice everything I love for anything or anybody. Besides, maybe Jesus is just testing us to see what's in us, to see what it is we really love—*for what, if anything, would we sacrifice our lives*.

Once upon a time God "tested" Abraham. (Genesis 22). God said to Abraham, *Kill me a son.*

Abe didn't hesitate. He set out for Mount Moriah to make a burnt offering of his beloved son. His beloved son Isaac went along. Isaac lugged the wood as Jesus would lug a cross two millennia later.

Isaac carried the wood. Abe carried the knife. Isaac mounted the altar. Abe raised the knife.

Now who's being tested?

In a flash an angel swept in and stopped Abe. (Some say the "angel" was Sarah, Isaac's mother.) Abe didn't kill his son. Still, just by being willing Abraham won the veneration of three historic religions.

Abe could have said, *Sorry, I won't do that! Find yourself another devotee.*

But he didn't say that. He went along. He unsheathed the knife.

Which, I imagine, prompted God to say: *I can't leave that guy alone for a minute. People like that must be watched. I mean, who in their right mind sacrifices their only-begotten son?!*

APOCALYPSE
September 15, 2019

My young friend is creating a new world in southern West Virginia. I'm not sure he would put it that way, but I do.

He grew up in Ona, just outside Huntington. He witnessed the apocalypse—the end of the world for people there. Mines, factories, railyards, businesses, homes, and hope abandoned. Lives left in ruins, leaning on opioids, alcohol, and disability checks.

My friend left. He attended Shepherd University and graduated in three years. Then he earned a master's degree in public affairs at Indiana State.

He could have gone anywhere. He went home. Back to the apocalypse.

My young friend's a believer. He believes that creative work can transform suffering. He was determined to create conditions for life to flourish in that dead zone. He had a seed of an idea.

He founded Coalfield Development Corporation, a nonprofit. He started with a small crew. Five at first. Then 10. And now, 10 years later, he's created more than 200 jobs for West Virginians.

This past Friday the Heinz Family Foundation awarded Brandon Dennison $250,000 for his work—*a transformative model of employment-based social enterprise helping to end generational poverty and create a new, diverse, and environmentally sustainable economy for West Virginia.*

Brandon's a believer. He believes the story of creation is always in play. After all, it's a parable of possibility and hope in times of despair. Through creative work, we can bring light out of darkness, life out of death, beauty out of chaos one day at a time. Time and time again.

I once had a friend who thought about creation all the time.

For 30 years this friend carried around in his pocket a self-drawn topographic map showing that "Creation" originated on his doorstep. The "Garden of Eden" once stood on land near his home along the Opequon Creek, he said. He had found precious stones there resembling those named in Genesis.

He figured if anybody should know the original location of Eden, the Pope should. So he took his map to the Vatican. The Pope was unavailable.

I saw my old friend the day before he died. He couldn't speak. He was holding the map next to his heart and smiling. Of course, we all thought he was crazy. But after he died, I thought: *What's so crazy about thinking creation can begin at your doorstep?*

RITA

September 29, 2019

To everything there is a season. A time to be born and a time to die.

Rita died on Monday. She was old, but she didn't die of old age. We requested euthanasia. The vet agreed it was time. She was 13 years old. Her hips were shot.

Still, she'd had her moments over the past few weeks. We'd tug her up onto those wobbly hind legs; she'd waddle off, tail wagging, and look back at us proudly. We noticed her gallant effort. And that made the road ahead harder.

If she had been able to talk, I would have asked her: Do you really want to go on living this way?

What kind of question is that?! Of course, I do! Ever notice how you limp more and more? Your right knee is shot. Is it your time to go?

Maybe it's good dogs can't talk.

To everything there is a season. A time for love and a time for hate.

Yes, I hate her for stealing our hearts, for trusting us with her life, and then forcing this upon us. All the way to the clinic, she said not a word. She sat on her haunches looking out the back window as though she'd never see this world again.

We opened the back hatch and lifted her in our arms. She gazed softly into our eyes. She knew we'd never do her any harm.

She had come to us from a rescue center as a scared and skittish puppy. It was a cold February day. We carried her into our warm house. Maya, our black lab, couldn't wait to sniff her butt and lick her ears. And just like that, Rita had a mate.

When Maya died a few years later, we adopted a black lab. Rita adored her younger sister, Lucy. She sniffed her butt and licked her ears. Lucy gladly returned the favor. Often.

When our infant twin granddaughters crawled on the floor, Rita would sniff their diapered butts and lick their ears. They hugged her hard and tight. She watched over them. They came to call her "Dog Mom."

Now our lovely Rita is gone. And Lucy is forlorn. She sits on her haunches and gazes softly into our eyes. And we into hers.

To everything there is a season. A time to speak and a time to be silent.

IS MARRIAGE HAZARDOUS?
October 6, 2019

Last Sunday I officiated a wedding at the Audubon Woodend Sanctuary in Chevy Chase. Beautiful bride. Handsome groom. Beaming parents. Gorgeous day. And lots of chirping birds.

I've officiated the marriages of brides and grooms for more than 40 years. Sometimes it's two brides; sometimes two grooms. Sometimes indoors; sometimes outdoors. Sometimes simple; sometimes extravagant.

The particulars of a ceremony may vary, but the result is the same: the creation of a covenant between two people witnessed by family and friends. A covenant is like a yoke. It keeps you working together, even when you'd rather wander off or quit.

Through all of life's vicissitudes, I will be with you. I will. I promise.

The covenant is sealed with vows, rings, and a kiss. And then the couple scurries up the aisle to majestic music.

Last Sunday the grinning bride and groom scurried up the aisle to the theme from *Star Wars*. I've officiated more than 250 weddings. That was a first.

And come to think of it, it's not a bad idea to introduce a battle motif into a wedding ceremony. It might not be romantic, but it's realistic. After all, marriage is not all bliss. It's been called "a crucible of change" for a reason. Which is why my last word to couples is always: *Learn how to forgive.*

I signed the marriage license, slipped it into my liturgy folder, and then forgot to hand it over. The next day, I put it into a large, flat, manila envelope, and took it to the Shepherdstown Post Office. The clerk set it on the scale and asked me: *Does this package contain anything liquid, hazardous, perishable, or breakable?*

He pointed to a screen with two buttons: YES. NO.

My finger flickered back and forth over the buttons. I stopped, took a deep breath, and stepped back.

Is there a problem, sir?

Yes, I think there may be. That envelope contains a marriage license.

JESUS SHAVES
October 13, 2019

That's funny. It wouldn't be funny if it were Bob, Moses, Muhammad, or Buddha shaving. JESUS SAVES. JESUS SHAVES. Funny!

HONK IF YOU LOVE CHEESES is funny, too, because there are a million bumper stickers taunting motorists to HONK IF YOU LOVE JESUS. I never honk. I'm pretty sure the Jesus I love isn't the one they love.

My Jesus is a fun guy. He rocks the boat.

He once told a fat-assed rich guy that it was easier for a camel to squeeze through the eye of a needle than for a fat-assed rich guy to get into heaven. *You gotta slim down, buddy, or you'll miss out on the good life.* Lots of knee slapping on that one, I bet.

Honk if you love Jesus.

I'm teaching a course at Shepherd University entitled "Jesus Before Christianity." It's a full class. A lot of us would like to know what Jesus was before he became a white evangelical Republican.

He was Jewish, that's what. He was born Jewish. He died Jewish.

His mother Mary (aka Miriam) was Jewish. And, no, she wasn't a "Catholic Jew" as one incredulous (Catholic) student insisted.

So, I've been downloading songs about Jesus. Jesus Was a Capricorn. The Rebel Jesus. Jesus Is Just Alright with Me. Jesus on the Mainline. We Need a Whole Lot More of Jesus (And a Lot Less Rock and Roll). And my favorite: They Ain't Makin Jews Like Jesus Anymore, by Kinky Friedman and the Texas Jewboys. (Yes, there is such a group.)

While googling Jesus I stumbled on "Jesus Shaves" by Paranoid Larry. (Yes, there is such a person). *Jesus loses his job in corporate America, becomes a welder, shaves twice a week, goes ice fishin' after church on Sunday, walks on water, bumbles into a date, marries Magdalena (from payroll), and has a daughter.*

I love that Jesus, too, and the blessing he offers.

> *Blessed are the ones who make peace, blessed are the ones who scrape by. Blessed are the ones living holy lives, and here's to the rest of us who try*

I never heard it that way from the Bible Jesus. I heard it from the one who shaves.

> *Here's to the rest of us who try.*

* * *

Listen to "Jesus Shaves" by the Roche Sisters on YouTube

COWSHIT
October 20, 2019

My four-year-old grandson Wyatt turns five in two weeks. I'm pretty sure that means no more blogging about him unless I get an attorney.

One hot day last month I picked him up in Boonsboro for his day at our house. After he's buckled snugly in his car seat in the back, he requests "boy rock." I know his preference, so I oblige with a carefully selected playlist that blasts us all the way to Shepherdstown.

Our weekly routine includes a carwash in the automatic bay at Whale of a Wash and then a quick stop in Food Lion for bananas, blueberries, and maybe a candy bar. After that, it's off to home but not through the shorter campus route because *I DON'T LIKE THAT WAY*. I once explained the advantages, but it didn't change his opinion.

At the car wash, I insert my credit card and make a selection. The door slowly rises. We enter and roll to a stop. The door closes behind us and suddenly we're met with a putrid smell.

Cowshit, says the passenger in the backseat.

What?

It's cowshit.

I can't disagree. His other grandparents live on a farm near Rohrersville. He's become an expert on cowshit.

After the wash, we pull around to Food Lion.

I don't want to go in there today.

That's OK, I say. I'll park by the door and dash in and out real quick. We only need some bananas. You can wait in the car.

But aren't you forgetting something, Grandy?

I don't think so. All we need are bananas. What am I forgetting?

The law.

As I said: This is my last blog about that guy.

OLD LETTERS
October 27, 2019

Last week during a round of decluttering I took the lid off a large box. It had sat unopened for nearly 40 years.

Funny how you can set something down meaning to get to it the next day, and then 40 years go by. I suppose a life can go by like that.

The box was stuffed with letters. The earliest was postmarked 1967. I was 20 years old, a junior in college.

Funny, I don't recall writing letters. Not one. Looking back I just can't see myself doing that—sitting down at a table, lifting a pen, writing on paper, folding it, tucking it in an envelope, sealing it, stamping it, and dropping it in a mailbox.

I can't believe I did that. The box says I did.

Apparently, I sent a letter, got a letter, and put it in a shoe box. Sent another, got another, and put it in the box. Over and over again until I needed a bigger box. At the time I didn't know I was curating a rare collection of a near extinct species.

Every time I moved, I took that box along—from Youngstown to Wheaton to Pasadena to Shepherdstown. I never re-read them. I just took them along, put them under my bed, or tucked them in the back of a closet like ashes in an urn. A memorial to friendships. A stone to touch.

In the box I found more than a hundred letters from old friends. Some deceased. I thought I'd read one, or two, or maybe three. I opened one, then another, and another, and another.

I tumbled down a rabbit hole into another world. We were all so very young then. Our nation hummed. The future was wide open. I read another. And one more. And one more.

I was a refugee. I could have lingered. I could have stayed. The past is such a refuge from the present.

I put the lid back on the box and climbed out of the hole, back into this world, back into now.

I don't know if I will ever touch those letters again. I know I won't toss them out. After all, the box isn't so big, and my closet has plenty of room.

Besides, there's still a whiff of perfume on a few of those letters.

A NEW DAY AT SPC
November 3, 2019

My former church found itself a new pastor. Last Sunday was her First. There will never be another First Sunday. I sent her my good wishes the day before.

We haven't met. I hope we will someday. I just wanted you to know that I've heard enough about you to be very pleased (and relieved) that you are SPC's next minister, joining a succession stretching back to 1743. I felt lucky and blessed to be part of such a company, serving an extraordinary community of saints and sinners. May your First Sunday be full of grace and delight. Knock 'em dead.

I am glad. Truly. But, I must confess, I'm a little sad, too. She gets to stand, kneel, and sit where I once stood, knelt, and sat. She gets to get a kick out of a congregation that once filled my soul with joy.

Funny how you think you're over something—the death of friend, a broken romance, a career—and then out of the blue you find an old letter, hear a certain song, or glimpse a bit of news, and just like that grief returns.

I had good reasons to retire, to leave that work and that household of faith. But reason has its limits. Just when you're moving briskly ahead, you get blindsided.

The happy news last week took me back to another time, back to my First Sunday—July 4, 1976. A church mostly empty every previous Sunday was full that day. *Let's go check out that long-haired, bearded dude from California and see what he's got.*

I didn't think my "First Sermon" from that historic pulpit was anything special. But that night all around Shepherdstown and all across America fireworks exploded. *What a start,* I thought.

The following Sunday the church was mostly empty. Never again would my sermons set off fireworks. (Although there were plenty of bombs.) The congregation was small but spunky. We walked together, fell in love, and plugged along through good times and hard times.

That was then. This is now.

I read the new pastor's "First Sermon" online. It was brilliant. She knocked 'em dead for sure. I heard fireworks that night. I hope she did, too.

May grace abound for the Reverend Gusti Linnea Newquist and her beloved flock. May their life together be invigorating, bodacious, long lasting, and peppered with great laughter.

YOGA SAVES!
November 10, 2019

I go to yoga the way a lot of people go to church. Which is to say, occasionally. And that means I feel guilty a lot of the time because I believe going to yoga is good for me. Yoga saves the body from corruption.

I didn't always believe that. I had to be convinced the way a sinner has to be convinced that Jesus saves a soul from corruption.

As luck would have it, in this town yoga has more evangelists than the churches do. Nearly every street corner has one.

I heard testimonies. I heard people say that through yoga they had been *born again*. OK. They didn't actually use *those words*. Still, I knew what they meant. Weight loss. Flexibility. Lower back pain relieved. Stability. Decluttered mind. Enlightenment.

I saw throngs going to yoga with mats under their arms the way Baptists carry Bibles to church. A few years ago, a friend said, *Come with me.*
I went.

It felt like being in church. Instead of pews, we sat on mats. Instead of prayers, we did poses. An instructor led us through a ritual. It took an hour. I learned how to sit, stand, twist, tuck, breathe, and bow to the divine in the other. Namaste.

Believing in Jesus will get you saved—or so it's been said. Believing in yoga won't get you anything. You gotta practice. It's not what you say. It's what you do.

Yoga is a yoke. It joins two things that tend to drift apart. I want to go more often—weekly, in fact. But I don't. And that's something yoga can't fix.

DEEP DARKNESS
December 1, 2019

Nightmares begone! Today is the First Sunday of Advent. There's a light up ahead. No more darkness. No more night.

> The people walking in darkness
> have seen a great light;
> on those living in the land of deep darkness
> a light has dawned.
> (Isaiah 9:2)

This year, more than ever, I want to believe it. I light a candle and hold my breath.

I look hard but I can't see a great light. I can't see through this darkness. I can't see the end of this national nightmare.

Country singer Hank Williams couldn't either. Different nightmare. But not that different.

Hank Williams knew darkness. He brought some of it on himself. Actually, a lot on himself. But not all. None of us does. The darkness finds us.

One night, Hank's mother saw something up ahead on the dark road. *Look*, she said to her son slumped beside her, *there's a light up ahead*. Hank looked up. He saw the light and later put it in a song. "No more darkness, no more night. I saw the light."

He sang that song everywhere. Everyone sang that song. It was sung at his funeral. It may be the most sung song in his catalogue. After all, we all long to see the light when we find ourselves living in a time of deep darkness.

One night in San Diego, Hank tumbled off the stage. Drunk. Again. It was the first of two shows.

Minnie Pearl put him in his Cadillac and drove around town singing "I saw the light," hoping to sober him up for the second show. Hank sang a few lines, then stopped. *Oh, Minnie*, he said, *I don't see no light.*

We can sing that song all night long. We can recite Isaiah every year. We can light a candle every day. That won't end our nightmare as far as I can see.

Light a candle anyway. Hope is the First Candle of Advent.

IMAGINE NO RELIGION
December 8, 2019

This is the Second Sunday of Advent. The first candle stands for hope. The second for faith. It may be hard to believe but—*Messiah is coming (back) to save us*. Or so we're told. Have faith.

Many Jews put it differently. Messiah has not and is not coming. A Messianic Age might come. But don't count on that either, they say. Better to plant a tree than hold your breath.

So you can either wait for Messiah or work toward the Messianic Age. Or both. Or neither.

According to the prophecy, the Messiah is something to long for because, well, for starters, the wicked will be annihilated—*he shall strike the earth with the rod of his mouth, and with the breath of his lips he shall kill the wicked* (Isaiah 11)—leaving righteous people like you and me alive to enjoy a peaceful world.

The lion and lamb will lie down together. Presumably, side by side—not one inside the other. But then, I don't expect vegan lions on this planet anytime soon. And last time I tuned in, the wicked were kicking the righteous silly.

Still, the prophet urges us to believe the improbable. And a certain poet urges us to imagine a new world.

Imagine no religion. Imagine there's no countries. Imagine all the people sharing all the world. It's easy if you try. Or, so he says.

Well, we can try. But imagining won't make it so. Religious people are everywhere. Yes, it might be easier if they weren't. But they are. We must learn to get along.

We can imagine no countries. But that won't make it so. Countries, nations, tribes, and parties are everywhere. We must learn to get along.

We can imagine no possessions, no greed, no hunger. And we can imagine the world as one. But that won't make it so. The world is not as one. In many places, hunger kills. And in most places, greed rules. War is still an answer.

Still, we can dream. We can believe in the peaceable kingdom. We can imagine the world as one. And we can imagine getting along.

Imagination is good. But it's not good enough.

Today is the Second Sunday of Advent. Light two candles. Take a deep breath. Then work on getting along with somebody.

JOY IN MUDVILLE
December 15, 2019

Advent is a Christian tradition steeped in Judaism. And Judaism is steeped in sorrow.

By the rivers of Babylon, we sat down and wept when we remembered Zion. (Psalm 137)

Zion stands for all that fills our hearts with joy. Zion is home, sweet home. Zion is where we long most to be. And when we lose it, we're as good as dead.

Jews and Christians both long for salvation. But each sees it a bit differently.

Someone once told me that Christians love football because it's about running over people and spiking the ball in the end zone and that Jews love baseball because it's about coming home after wandering in unfriendly territory.

I don't know about that. But I do know this: Advent calls us back home.

The first candle stands for Hope. The second for Faith. The third for Joy.

The third candle burns for those in exile, wandering a long way from home. It burns for those who dwell in sorrow. A country lost. A loved one dead. A dream crushed. A life unlived.

Today's a good day to lift up your heart. Behold! A road in the wilderness. Stand up. Take a step.

The eyes of the blind shall be opened, and the ears of the deaf unstopped. The lame shall leap like a deer, and the tongue of the dumb sing for joy. The ransomed of the LORD shall return, and come to Zion with singing. Everlasting joy shall be upon their head. Sorrow and sighing shall flee away. (Isaiah 35)

Some wait for the LORD. Some wait for Messiah. Some wait for better weather. Some wait for the next election. And some just start walking—for as it turns out, *the road is made by walking*. As the 16th century Franciscan friar Giovanni put it in his Christmas letter:

> The gloom of the world
> is but a shadow,
> behind it, yet, within our reach,
> is joy.
> Take Joy.

According to Ernest Lawrence Thayer's ballad "Casey at the Bat," there was no joy in Mudville when the mighty Casey struck out. No one made it home that day. But it wasn't the end of the world. Casey would walk to the plate again and again. One day joy would come to Mudville.

Today's a good day to light three candles and remember what you long to be. And then walk that way.

HOPE FOR OUR COUNTRY
December 22, 2019

Today is the fourth Sunday of Advent. The fourth candle stands for IMPEACHMENT.

Well, maybe not on every Advent wreath in this country. But at least half. On the other half the fourth candle still stands for PEACE.

World peace would be nice, but this year we'd settle for peace in our country. It could break out anywhere—even in Martinsburg.

This Tuesday evening past, the Eve of Impeachment, I stood with a gaggle of citizens on the four corners of King and Queen streets in Martinsburg. We stood under the glow of Christmas lights woven around lamp posts.

Any other year such a gaggle of bundled, gloved, and shivering souls would be singing "Joy to the World." Not this year. We had not come out to sing carols.

The night was cold. The wind bitter. Our mission formidable. And yet there was good cheer. Alone, we might despair. Together, we could believe.

Even when a counter group sprang at us flaunting an American flag in our faces, we didn't flinch, fight, or fuss. We stood our ground. They eventually stopped prancing and stood their ground.

We were standing for one thing that night. They were standing for something else. Still, they were standing with us, shivering in the same cold wind. For they too love this embattled country.

Love is affection. But it's more than that. It's also warm regard for the other, even when we don't like them. You don't have to be pure of heart to love. And therein lies hope for our country.

Today is the fourth Sunday of Advent. Light the candles of HOPE, FAITH, JOY, and PEACE. For Christmas is nigh. Love is abornin'.

The curse shall be lifted. Blessings shall flow. Wonders shall never cease.

LOVE IN VEGAS
January 12, 2020

Our twin granddaughters live in Albuquerque. They're 11 years old, just this side of puberty and corruptibility.

Over Christmas break we took them to Las Vegas to see "Love" at the Mirage—a Cirque du Soleil tsunami of kinetic exuberance splashed through a pulsating Beatles' soundscape—from "Get Back" to "All You Need Is Love" plus 24 other songs. Ninety minutes of bliss.

We first experienced "Love" eight years ago. I was born again. Raptured. Taken away like Lucy in the Sky with Diamonds.

The moment the show ended, we said: *We gotta bring Angie and Paula here someday.*

We drove all day. We drove through blowing snow and freezing rain. We drove 575 miles, arriving just after sundown on the fourth day of Christmas.

VIVA LAS VEGAS, *baby!*

Nobody puts the MERRY in Christmas like Vegas. Sparkling lights, jingle jangle round the clock, and, of course, GAY APPAREL—drummers drumming, pipers piping, swans a-swimming, lords a-leaping, ladies dancing, shirtless Santa's, spike-heeled angels, and, oh yeah, dreary souls wrapped in sleeping bags on sidewalks.

Joy to the world. Peace on earth. Goodwill to all.

A street corner preacher shouted through a bull horn. REPENT. YOU MUST BE BORN AGAIN.

It was a sermon no one would hear. No one came near. Why would we care? *We're walking streets of gold, baby!*

No one was saved.

Next morning we ate breakfast on the Strip. The girls spied a Coca-Cola retail store and rushed in. Ten thousand items blazoned with the company logo; likewise in the M&M's, Hershey's, and Reese's stores. Their heads spun. Their eyes popped. Their wallets opened.

We strolled past Cartier, Dior, Gucci, Prada, Valentino, and more. The girls took it all in stride while I was wishing we'd all get born again. Born Amish. Quickly! Before it's too late.

I once had a crush on the Amish. *Live simply that others may simply live.* I wanted to. Still do. Sometimes.

We crossed a pedestrian bridge from one emporium to another. A bedraggled man played an accordion for tips. Yet another beggar.

Where do they all come from?

We bustled by.

Suddenly, Little P, the youngest of the twins and a fledging mandolin player, turned back. She pulled a dollar out of her wallet and laid it in the musician's hat.

Yes, love is all you need.

And it's way more than a show in Vegas.

MAGICAL MYSTERY TOUR
January 26, 2020

Once a month in my church days, I would lead a song and prayer service with several others from my congregation at Canterbury nursing home. We'd sing a few songs, read a few Bible verses, say a prayer, and then greet the dozen or so souls one by one as we left.

We knew that any given greeting might be the last. Death was no stranger in that place.

At one service while singing "Swing Low, Sweet Chariot," we got to the line *I looked over Jordan and what did I see,* and I heard a new voice proclaim: A BAND OF COWBOYS COMIN' AFTER ME.

At every service from then on, we would stop singing at that point and let her have the floor. A BAND OF COWBOYS COMIN' AFTER ME.

She beamed. We beamed. The whole world beamed.

Well, why not? Whatever gets you through the night—or over Jordan—it's all right, it's all right, it's all right.

A few services later, she was gone—her spot empty (except for a pair of spurs).

Over the next couple of years, I told that story to several parishioners facing imminent death. It got a laugh out of them. So I'd say to them: *Tell me what you see when you get close enough to look over Jordan.*

Michelle told me she saw buffalo. Then she smiled. She died three days later.

Bill told me he saw breasts, large breasts. I held his smile and kept myself from looking at his wife. When I did look, she was smiling. He died that night.

Cowboys. Buffalo. Breasts. The sky is not the limit. Who knows what you might see.

Last month Paula and I took our granddaughters to see the Cirque du Soleil's *Love* in Las Vegas. Ninety enrapturing minutes of Beatles songs. I thought: *If I get to choose when and where to die, it would be right here, immersed in this soundscape with my family and friends sitting close by.*

And that thought led to another. *Maybe, just maybe, on the day I look over Jordan, I might see a flowery bus rolling up, rolling up to take me away on a Magical Mystery Tour.*

I'm not looking for that bus at the moment. I have a dear friend who is.

No ticket required.

BON VOYAGE, DEAR FRIEND
February 2, 2020

This past Tuesday the Magical Mystery Tour bus came for my friend. I didn't think it would arrive so soon. I didn't have a chance to say goodbye. If I had, I would have wished him bon voyage.

I just can't accept that death is a full stop. Not for anybody. And certainly not for him. I can't think of him as gone. I might as well think of the sun as gone.

I never had a dull encounter with him. Every encounter—no matter how short or long—was exuberant. His body radiated joy, even mirth. His soul never flickered. It's hard to imagine him dead when I can't even imagine him asleep. Ever.

Years ago, when he was downsizing for a move, he gifted me one of his watercolor paintings. A sagging school bus painted blue, parked beside a shabby house. Behind the bus three scruffy men warm their hands over a fire, flames flicking out of a rusted oil drum. Above the windshield in the destination panel of the bus are two faded words: JESUS SAVES.

Every time I look at this, he said, *I think of you. I don't know why. I sometimes see those three men back there as the three wise men. I don't know if that house behind them is theirs. And I don't know if that's their bus. Or if it still runs.*

He painted those men, the house, the fire, and the bus and still didn't know. I don't either.

The painting hung in my church office for 20 years. When I retired, I took it home. It's here in this room beside me as I write.

I don't know where the dead go or if they go at all. No one knows. But we can imagine. We can dream. We can sing. We can paint.

Joe was an artist. He knew there was more than he could paint. He knew there was more than he could say. And he knew there was more than he could know.

I don't know if he got on that Magical Mystery Tour bus.

I imagine he did.

SYMPATHY FOR THE JOKER
(Just in time for the Oscars)
February 9, 2020

I saw "Joker" last week. Before the (sociopathic) "Joker" became Batman's notorious nemesis, he was just Arthur Fleck. Arthur has a backstory. He had an unhappy childhood.

I felt sorry for him.

I saw "Judy" last week. Judy Garland died of a drug overdose at age 47. Judy has a backstory. She had an unhappy adolescence.

I felt sorry for her.

I saw "Parasite" last week. Kun-sae went on a clever-wielding murderous rampage. Kun-sae has a backstory. He had an unhappy existence living like a rat in a sub-basement.

I felt sorry for him.

Everybody has a backstory. It takes interest and time to learn it. It takes compassion.

It doesn't always lead to exoneration. But it can lead to understanding. And understanding can lead to empathy.

As the Buddha said: *Be kind to everyone. You never know what another is dealing with.*

I've been told that certain people on the other side are evil. Not merely incompetent, ignorant, or insecure. Evil. Irredeemably so. No backstory worth learning. No humanity.

Maybe so. I don't know them.

But I know the Joker. I walked two hours in his floppy shoes.

He had no father to speak of. Mom's boyfriend had cursed him, beat him, and tied him to a radiator. Arthur landed in an asylum. He got out never knowing what got him in.

He lived with his unhappy mother in a threadbare flat. Time and again, she'd say to him: "Happy, your purpose is to bring laughter and joy to this world." (She always called him "Happy.")

Ma, I'm not happy! I haven't been happy for one minute of my entire life!!

And yet, he played the clown. ("Put on a happy face and smile.") He tried to be funny.

You're not funny. Your jokes aren't funny. You're a joke.

A person can take only so much. Only so much humiliation, rejection, and hurt.

Arthur had taken enough.

It was too late for therapy. It was too late for pills. It was too late for hugs.

It was time to be his magnificent, maleficent self.

I'm sympathetic.

Still, I lock my doors at night. And then look over my shoulder.

SAVING JESUS
February 16, 2020

Before Jesus got converted into a white evangelical Republican, he was a child of Judaism, working for social justice.

(No justice. No peace.)

He was hardly original. Not even in death. The Romans crucified thousands of Jewish young men. Crucifixion was a deterrent to terrorism.

(We have other methods.)

Jesus wasn't the first Jewish reformer. Others advocated what Jesus advocated. Others were inclusive. The holy (wholesome) way is hardly a secret. It's shouted from every mountain top and in every religion.

LOVE ONE ANOTHER.

The Roman Empire wanted world peace (and would kill anyone who got in the way). Everybody wants world peace—except the military industrial congressional university research complex slurping at the trough.

(War may be easier to stop than greed.)

By the first century certain beleaguered Jews under the heel of Rome were sick and tired of a certain so-called Son-of-God-Prince-of-Peace-Savior-of-the-World, and, yes, born-of-a-virgin emperor (Augustus).

Evangelists (messengers) were spreading a gospel (evangel) to the empire's subjects: *Give your loyalty (and taxes) to Caesar, and all will be well. You will be safe. No threat will come near you. The borders will be secure.*

(Lies. Lots of lies.)

In Jesus, some saw a different kind of power, a different way toward peace—a deep truth resurrected, incarnated, made flesh. *Feed the hungry, heal the sick, love enemies, drop grudges, welcome everybody to the table.*

(In that kingdom, love, not fear, would rule.)

And thus, "Jesus" was raptured into human imagination—transfigured into an icon of compassion, a counter to greed and revenge. *I will love my enemies even if it kills me.*

A handful of subversives created an alternative gospel—a different Son of God, Prince of Peace, Savior of the World, and, why not, born of a virgin, too—to counter the empire's myth.

It was an existential choice: Caesar OR Christ. (At least until the empire co-opted Christ.)

This spring I'm teaching a class at Shepherd University: *Jesus Before Christianity*. (Hint, hint: He was Jewish.)

Jesus was a Jew, I once told a Catholic friend.

No way!! How could that be?!

It could be—and was—because his mother was Jewish.

Well, then, she must have been a Catholic Jew!

No. She. Wasn't. And I should know. I'm an expert on these matters.

(Not really.)

Still, I'm teaching a class and trying to save Jesus from my former tribe, American evangelicals, and their new emperor.

LOOKING FOR JESUS
February 23, 2020

I know a lot about Jesus. More than a lot of people. He's been a lifelong obsession. (*Lord help me Jesus, I can't quit you.*)

What's a neurotic to do?

I know what I'm doing. I'm teaching a class.

(*Jesus Before Christianity* at Shepherd University Lifelong Learning.)

It took me a while to realize I could package my neurosis for the benefit of others. I mean, why be selfish with your obsessions?

I've been looking for Jesus most of my life. Much to my surprise, the closer I got, the less there was. Like a mirage. Still, a mirage can get you to a place you might otherwise miss—if you keep trudging.

My evangelical friends told me that knowing *about* Jesus wasn't good enough.

That won't save you, Randy. You got Jesus in your head. You need Jesus in your heart. Do you walk and talk with him? Is he your friend?

Actually, no. I don't have any invisible friends. I used to. When I was five.

I tried to conjure up Jesus so I could walk and talk with him (on the mainline, in the garden, on my pillow). It didn't work. It felt childish.

(*Childlike* faith is one thing. *Childish* is another.)

As it turns out, I couldn't bring myself to believe in Jesus in that way. But I kept trudging.

And then one day, out of the blue, a Jewish friend told me: *I don't believe in Jesus. I believe with him. I believe in the power of love.*

Lightning struck.

Those Jews! Why didn't I think of *that* long ago?!

I guess it helps to have a 2,000-year head start.

THE GREENING OF SOUTHERN WEST VIRGINIA
March 1, 2020

I spent this past weekend in Huntington. I was asked to give a boost to 50 some men and women working with Coalfield Development Corporation.

CDC was founded by Shepherd University graduate Brandon Dennison in 2010. It aims to revitalize southern West Virginia one graduation, one job, one family, one green plant at a time.

We started with a bluegrass standard: "Working on a Building." Last verse—*I'd quit my preachin' and work on a buildin' with you.*

(I had other reasons to quit my preaching, but having time for these spunky men and women is one.)

I told them I was a grandson of a Pennsylvania coal miner. My grandfather died from a mining accident with no compensation afforded his family of four girls and three boys. It left a chip on my father's shoulder.

The capitalists will always take advantage of the working man, he once told me.

His chip fell on me.

(Poverty, exploitation, and enslavement are not conditions of nature. People create those. Sympathy is nice. But repairs and reparations are necessary for justice to prevail.)

I spoke of growing up in Youngstown—of abandoned mills, broken homes, shattered lives, opiods.

We listened to a song made popular by Bob Marley.

> *By the rivers of Babylon*
> *we sat down*
> *and there we wept*
> *when we remembered Zion.*

We paused and remembered southern West Virginia. What was. What is. What could be.

I told them a parable from the Great Ancestors.

Once upon a time the Creator stumbled upon a real mess. Chaos and darkness. Let's see what can be done, said the Creator.

The Creator got to work—separating light from darkness, land from water, plotting, plowing, and planting—one day at a time right on through the work week until conditions were ripe for life to flourish.

Plants and animals arose from the earth, including one with divine-like powers to create and destroy. And, behold is was good.

Or was it?

The parable leaves us with a question: *How will we use our powers?*

We listened to Bruce Springsteen's "My City of Ruins."

> *Rise up, rise up.*
> *With these hands. With these hands.*
> *Come on, come on.*
> *Rise up.*

Then they shared stories of personal tragedies and of working to rebuild from the ruins. To bring light out of darkness. To mend the world.

It's never perfect. But it's good. And good ain't bad.

HILLBILLY HOT DOGS
(A Love Story)
March 8, 2020

There actually is such a place. It's just outside Huntington on the Ohio River Road heading north. You can't miss it. There's a hand-painted sign. WE GOT THE WEENIES. The "dining room" is two school buses jammed together.

It's what's called a "point of destination." Which means it's not on your way to somewhere else. Or next to another place you happen to be. There's nothing else out there. Which means you actually thought about it and still went.

My friend (who shall remain nameless) took his prom date there. Engagements have been announced there. Weddings have been held there. (You get a "Weenie Wedding Certificate.")

As far as I know, babies coulda been born there. (There's a Bouncin' Baby Combo on the menu.) People could easily die there, too. I saw hefty patrons huffing, shoe-horning into seats.

The menu nicely accommodates death.

For $19.99, you can order the Homewrecker: a 15-inch, 1-pound weenie with 2 pounds of toppings, including jalapeños, sautéed peppers & onions, nacho cheese, Habaneros, chili sauce, mustard, slaw, lettuce, tomato, and shredded cheese.

Or, if you need quicker results, you can upgrade to the Widow Maker for $32.50. That would be a 30-inch, 2-pound weenie, and 4 pounds of toppings!

Paula and I went there for lunch. Our whole food, plant-based diet took a back seat and turned its head.

We didn't want to overly jeopardize our mortality (or marriage) so we ordered lite fare (two regular weenies with chili sauce, onion, mustard, French fries, and pop). I know sugary pop isn't good for you, so I got a Devil Anse (Hatfield) IPA instead. (WE GOT THE BREWSKIES)

That morning I had made a presentation to 50-some men and women working with Coalfield Development Corporation to revitalize southern West Virginia. I had spoken of our divine-like capacity to transform suffering—large and small, regional and personal—into something whole and wholesome through creative work.

Creative work takes many forms. It could be deadly serious. Or fun and funky (and only marginally wholesome).

In the fall of 1999, a certain hillbilly came back home with his California bride, put up a 12-by-16 shed on the land where he'd grown up, and started selling hotdogs. A dream come true. Sonny and Sharie got married there three days later.

They've been renewing their wedding vows there every year since.

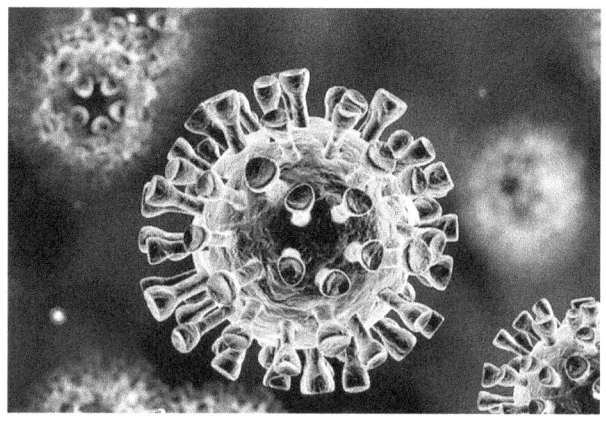

AN ACT OF GOD?
March 15, 2020

Is the coronavirus pandemic an "act of God" as some claimed HIV/AIDS, Hurricane Katrina, the Black Death, and the Mt. Vesuvius eruption were?

So far, I haven't heard anyone say so. But then, Jerry Falwell is dead. The pope knows better. And the doddering Pat Robertson has "underlying conditions." He could be next. He's sweatin' Bibles.

Back in the day, when I was an apologist for theism, the categorical claim "act of God" made me bristle. What's up with that? Does God only wreak havoc? Why are only floods, hurricanes, earthquakes, and pestilences "acts of God"? What about a gorgeous day? Can't that be an "act of God"?

Surely God needs a better PR department, I thought. Where were the Mad Men when God needed them?!

I heard of an Australian fisherman who lost his boat to a lightning strike. It wasn't a leisure boat. It was his livelihood.

The insurance company refused payment since the strike was an "act of God." The fisherman sued the church hierarchy. After all, they claimed to be God's representatives on earth.

The case went to court.

For thousands of years, God was the only explanation for every unknown. And for just as long, God was the only hope of mitigation. Many looked to God for deliverance from pandemics and pestilences. Now most of us look to science for explanations and mitigation.

Still, I'm not ruling God out of this pandemic. Not quite yet.

Let's say this pandemic is an "act of God" like "the plagues of Egypt." Who, then, would be the blustery, belligerent, bully Pharaoh, who thinks he's all powerful and all knowing, holding sway over the world? Who needs to be humbled?

I'm pretty sure it's not Tom Hanks.

BIRDS ARE BUDDHISTS
March 22, 2020

I let the cat out this morning. She never bolts out the door. She ponders the risk. Twitches her tail, once, twice, and again. Moves one foot forward. Then another. And finally scurries out and settles quickly under the bird feeder hanging from a low branch.

The birds above fall silent, ponder her presence. She crouches, ready to fly up the tree. The birds calculate the risk and restart their song. They have wings even though they don't know it.

In other trees the birds are merrily chirping. The grass is greening and soon will need mowing. Cut down but not for long. Each blade will rise again, stretching toward the sun.

The soil is warming. Worms are squirming. No one has to tell them the early bird is out to catch them. Still, they can't sleep in. No one told them that's an option. They can't shelter in place. They have things to do and places to go.

The cat's out.

The birds chirp.

The worms squirm.

The sun rises.

It will shine on the righteous and the wicked today. It can't discriminate. Doesn't know how. Never has. I know this but seldom acknowledge it. Today I press my hands together in front of my heart and bow.

Namaste.

The ash trees in my woods are dying. They don't know what's eating them. They don't know a pest has doomed them. They don't know a chainsaw is coming.

Their branches are bare. Leaf buds show their faces. They don't know their predecessors lie dead on the ground beneath them. They don't know the past; can't dwell on it. All they know is this moment, this chance to be alive. To be here now, even as they become something else.

The birds gather on those sickly branches and chant. Birds can't see the future. Dread is unknown. They sing in this moment, in this place. It's all they know, if they know even that. Birds are born Buddhists.

A friend told me you can see God under a leaf. I don't know about that. I don't know that God is even God like that.

But I know the sacred. It's in all things. There's no one name for it. It asks for nothing but reverence. And gratitude.

I told my friend, if you can't see the sacred in a leaf, there's no use looking under it.

ZOOM
(A love story)
March 29, 2020

This past Wednesday was my first time in a Zoom room. I didn't zoom in. I crept in, one baby step at a time.

Meanwhile, school children all around the world blithely zoom in and out of such rooms. Good for them. I'm old. I don't zoom anywhere. (Beam me up, Scotty. I can't move!)

I got in. Somehow. I fiddled with the mouse (*here a click, there a click, everywhere a click-click*). I looked up and—lo, and behold—I saw a gallery of 24 beaming faces, like Hollywood Squares squared.

Magic.

The Zoom website says it's "super natural." (*I don't know about that. But it's not far from "miraculous."*)

This was a test run for my Shepherd University Lifelong Learning class, "Jesus Before Christianity." The class begins in earnest next week. Four weeks ago, the virus doomed it. Zoom saved it. We are together again, face-to-face, without touching.

Zoom, I found out, is a contagion. Everybody's getting it.

It connects teachers with students, bosses with employees, committee chairs with members, parishioners with pastors, physicians with patients, grandparents with grandchildren, lovers with each other.

Zoom is saving the world from a worse fate. It keeps us together while apart. All because engineers are lovers, too.

Zoom originated in China. Well, I should say, in a certain Chinese boy's head.

Thirty years or so ago, Yuán Zhēng, an engineering student at Shandong University of Science and Technology was in love. To see his girlfriend, he had to take a train. It took hours and hours. Ten to be exact.

There's got to be a quicker way to see her. If only I had a way to zoom out there.

He started dreaming in algorithms.

Yuán married his girlfriend, moved to Silicon Valley, and went to work on his dream. After all, the world is full of lovers longing to be together when apart.

Yuán is now a billionaire. When asked what he requires of those who work for him, he has a one-word answer: *Care. I want all my employees to care for others. It's not our slogan. It's our practice.*

I once thought of China as paper, fireworks, pagodas, dragons, Confucius, the Tao, the Great Wall. I still do. But I've added two other words: Zoom. And love.

Love makes the world go round. Zoom keeps it from falling apart.

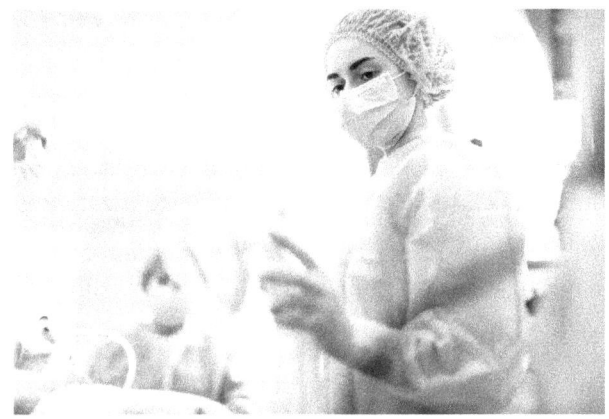

WORLD WAR III

April 5, 2020

So this is it. World War III. Every nation on the battlefield again. But this time, everyone is on the same side, fighting to eradicate a virus. I never pictured that war that way.

Combat troops are armed with cotton masks, disposable gowns, rubber gloves, thermometers, and syringes—fighting to save lives. Everyone on the same side.

(Is it too early to thank the virus?)

The whole world is endangered. The threat is unprecedented, we're told.

The dinosaurs might disagree.

One day, in the Mesozoic era, an asteroid 6 miles wide came flaming out of the blue across the continent at 50,000 miles per hour. A dinosaur casually munching leaves from a tall tree looked up. Its eyes popped. Its jaw dropped. Its heart stopped.

What was that?!

It was the end of the world.

But it wasn't the end of the planet.

Another world arose. After all, resurrection isn't just an Easter story. It's the planet's story. And every person's story. We die in one world and are born in another. Over and over again.

There are many worlds on this one planet. And worlds within worlds.

The planet is given.

The world is made.

We now have a chance to make a different kind of world. More healthy. More just. More peaceful. More at home. More content with less.

The world will always be many countries, many nations, many people, many colors, many languages, many religions, many passions.

Different. Diverse. Distinct.

Still, we can all be on the same side, fighting to eradicate hunger, poverty, illiteracy, bigotry, and greed.

We don't have to imagine the world working together as one.

We've seen it.

EASTER 2020
(I saw Jesus today)
April 12, 2020

I saw Jesus in the tomb today. (I thought it would be empty, but it wasn't.)

I saw Jesus in the morgue today, lying on a slab in an unzipped body bag.

I saw Jesus in the ICU, on a ventilator, gasping for air.

I saw Jesus in a corridor, writhing on a gurney as it rolled past.

I saw Jesus in a line, six feet behind the next person, waiting to be tested.

I saw Jesus in the ER, wearing a mask, a swab stick between his gloved fingers.

I saw Jesus in a ward, scrubbing door knobs, sponging counters, and scouring bedpans.

I saw Jesus in a tent, stooping over a cot, mopping a fevered brow.

I saw Jesus in a grocery store, restocking shelves with bread (and wine).

I saw Jesus in a laboratory, running vaccine trials with a team of scientists.

I saw Jesus in a synagogue, alone, weeping, a prayer shawl draped over his shoulders.

I saw Jesus at home, reading *Winnie the Pooh* to children online. (For such is the kingdom of heaven!)

I saw Jesus sitting on the porch, in a swing, wearing earbuds, rocking back and forth, smiling ear to ear. A baby slept on his lap.

I saw Jesus in the garden, kneeling, weeding, and humming an Easter hymn. I think it was "Thine Is the Glory," but it could have been "Here Comes the Sun." (I saw three earthworms wiggling in his soiled hand.)

A kitten crept by slowly, softly, stalking a butterfly.

A bunny hopped by.

A robin chirped.

RESURRECTION
(A week later)
April 19, 2020

I saw Jesus napping in a hammock in my backyard. A transistor radio lay on his chest. A baseball game was on. Orioles and Yankees.

First inning.

I stepped softly past the hammock, slipped around the pond (frogs croaked), and into a field of flowers.

Butterflies fluttered.

I picked three fistfuls of bluebells and put them in a jar. I walked to my neighbor's house. The shades were pulled.

(Her son was buried yesterday. No one came.)

I set the jar on the porch.

(A blackbird limped across the porch, gasping with each halting step. One wing was broken. It stood still, trembling, uncertain. I kneeled on the step, watching, a vigil to keep. The sun was slowly sinking down. The silent bird shuddered, fluffed its feathers, rose on its toes, lifted both wings, and flew away.)

I walked back to my yard.

The hammock was empty.

The radio was on.

Last inning.

The Orioles won.

CRUCIFIXION
(Lest Easter make us forget!)

April 26, 2020

I saw Jesus hanging from a cross.

Strange tree.

(10,000 other bodies were hanging along the Roman highway.)

I saw Jesus in a boxcar, a yellow star over his heart. I saw Jesus in a camp, down in a hole, digging. I saw Jesus in the Holocaust Museum, shoeless, weeping.

I saw Jesus in court, in the dock, the public defender asleep. I saw Jesus in prison, clad in orange, shackles on his ankles. I saw Jesus on death row, praying, eating his last meal.

I saw Jesus in Salem, lashed to a stake, on fire. I saw Jesus in a women's shelter, face battered. I saw Jesus in New York City, marching with suffragists.

I saw Jesus in Wyoming, body charred, tethered to a fence. I saw Jesus open a closet door, and another, and another. I saw Jesus dancing in a gay pride parade, smiling, waving, blowing kisses.

I saw Jesus in Mexico, following a coyote across the river. I saw Jesus picking strawberries, stooping, stooping, stooping in a cloud of pesticide. I saw Jesus in a union hall, painting a sign.

I saw Jesus sitting on a railroad track, facing a munitions train. I saw Jesus on Wall Street, toting a sledge hammer. I saw Jesus on the White House lawn, handcuffed, a flag burning at his feet.

I saw Jesus in the belly of a ship, crossing the Atlantic. I saw Jesus in the back of a bus. I saw Jesus in Selma, crossing a bridge, fire in his eyes.

I saw Jesus in a garden, under a stark tree, arms raised to heaven.

I saw Jesus in church, a noose around his neck.

I saw Jesus hanging from a tree.

(10,000 other bodies were hanging in the dark woods.)

Strange fruit.

* * *

Listen to Billy Holiday's rendition of "Strange Fruit" on YouTube.

RESURRECTION SEX
(Breaking news!)
May 3, 2020

Years ago when I was a preacher, I read the appointed lessons for the day from the pulpit. One Sunday I was reading a gospel episode (Matt. 22:23-33) in which the Sadducees put a challenge to Jesus. (The Sadducees did not believe in resurrection. Jesus and the Pharisees did.)

The Sadducees were a conservative sect. Businessmen, you might say. Most Jews at the time despised the Roman occupying forces, but the Sadducees figured *if you can't beat 'em, join 'em.*

The Sadducees got cushy jobs with the occupiers. Life was comfortable. When life is that good, you don't need a better future. You're living it now. Only desperate people long for justice in the future.

A smattering of resurrection speculation appears in the Hebrew Prophets. Ezekiel, for example, says: *These dry bones will rise up someday. Our crushed people will be restored to a good and splendid life.*

The Sadducees didn't think much of the Prophets. They thought only the Torah, the Five Books of Moses, was valid. And they didn't see any resurrection mentioned there. For them, any talk of resurrection was silly and unfounded.

Jesus thought differently. Resurrection was in the cards.

So the Sadducees put him on the spot, hoping to stump him in public.

A woman married. Her husband died. So she married her husband's brother in order to bear an heir for her deceased husband, as the law required. That husband died without an heir. She married the next brother in line. He died and so on through seven brothers. So in the resurrection, *whose wife will she be?*

(The Sadducees chuckled. Jesus smiled.)

She won't be anybody's wife. In the Resurrection there is no marriage.

I'd read that verse many times. But suddenly I saw something I'd never seen before. I paused. (Should I say it out loud?) (No!) (But it's...) (Don't!) I couldn't help myself. I said it out loud. From the pulpit!

Notice: Jesus said no marriage. He didn't say no sex.

Three days later I got two letters.

One berated me for endorsing sex outside marriage.

The other applauded me. It was from a harried, single mom raising four children.

I've been going to church all my life and that's the first time I've heard good news. Thank you.

There's more than one way to read the Bible.

TRUST SCIENCE
May 24, 2020

"In God We Trust" declares the American motto.

And what god would that be, pray tell? Last I counted there were lots. Can I pick one?

Can I pick the one who lifts up the poor and pulls the mighty from their thrones, the one who builds bridges and tears down walls, the one who welcomes refugees and forgives debts, the one who orders military machines crushed and refashioned into plows?

No! You can't pick that one, silly! That's not the god "we" have in mind. Not. At. All.

So then, pray tell, who do you mean by "we"? Not me, apparently. Not most of us. No one asked *us* what motto we wanted. If they had, we might have said: *In Love We Trust*. That would be nice. But *In Science We Trust* wouldn't be bad either.

I, for one, trust science.

I trust the priesthood of science for our salvation. I trust the wizards of science, scoping petri dishes, testing vaccines. I trust the prophets of science, even when they prophesy doom and gloom. Truth is not always convenient or soothing.

(False prophets of old proclaimed, "Peace, Peace," when there was no peace.)

I trust governors who trust science. I trust mayors who trust science. I trust shopkeepers who trust science. I trust neighbors who trust science.

I don't trust politicians who bow to mammon and polls. I don't trust Bible-waving preachers with flag pins on their lapels. I don't trust quacks. I don't trust a president with his nose in the air one minute, his head in the sand the next, and now hydroxychloroquine on his breath.

To be sure, scientists get things wrong. Sometimes the priesthood of science inflicts harm. After all, among them are frauds, bullies, and narcissists. I don't expect perfection or piety, for under every lab coat is a human being.

Still, I trust scientists to make things right when they get things wrong. Unlike religious dogmatists, scientists are skeptical, even of themselves and their findings. I like that. That's humility. And so I trust the (truly) catholic community of scientists to be forthright, honest, self-correcting, and unselfish.

None of us can know everything or much of anything at all by ourselves. So we must trust someone, especially when the stakes are high.

I trust scientists. And poets who see what science can't.

HOW TO STOP A REBELLION
May 31, 2020

I have two grandsons. They live in Boonsboro. Far enough not to see (or hear) them everyday. Close enough to fetch them now and then.

Of course, they're welcome anytime. But they come only at certain times.

And on those certain times, I stop them at the door to review the house rules, like Moses delivering 10 behavioral modification rules to the Israelites before entering the Promised Land. I count off seven rules on seven fingers (leaving three available for new rules.)

Walk, don't run.

Quiet voices.

No fighting.

Clean up your messes.

Ask permission before opening the refrigerator.

Take a nap after lunch.

And when you see Mimi, ask her: *How can I help you today?*

Considering the boys' ages, I leave out no fornication, no adultery, and no other gods (before me). I also don't consider stoning as an enforcement. Instead it's *Sit on that chair and don't move! Keep that up and there'll be no orange Creamsicle for you!*

For a long spell, Eli and Wyatt took the house rules in stride, without complaint. And then one day they marched up the stairs from the basement and stood before me, hands on hips. "Grandy, we don't like your rules." (Apparently they had been discussing the rules over the Lego table.)

"Which rules don't you like?"

"All of them!"

I'm no king, prime minister, or president. But I got a sense of what it might feel like to be one facing a rebellion.

I was proud of my grandsons. I was glad they conspired to rebel against authority. My heart sang. (I never dreamed of such a thing until I was at least 20.)

"Well, boys, I'm glad you told me. But if you don't want to follow my house rules, I will take you home now and you won't get that Creamsicle I promised."

They looked at each other, turned around, hopped down the stairs, and went back to the Legos. Without a fuss.

It only took an orange Creamsicle to squelch the rebellion.

My heart sank.

EXPLOSIVE DEVICE
June 7, 2020

On Monday, June 1, 2020, at 7:10 p.m. Eastern Time, the president of the United States of America held up a Bible in front of St. John's Episcopal, a historic white church across from the White House.

The Episcopal Church, formerly the Church of England, was once bound to the King of England, as were the colonies, until protests by patriots led to the mustering of British troops, which led to riots, looting, and burning, which led to more troops, which led to a bloody revolution, which transformed the colonies into a sovereign nation.

The king lost his colonies and his church, but he still had his Bible.

King George III revered the King James Bible. The colonists read it. ("Rebellion to tyrants is obedience to God!")

While posing in front of the church, the president thrust the Bible upward, careful to keep the book level with his head, not above it. (His attorney general had told him nothing could be above him.)

The president may have intended to send a message of defiance by mimicking the Black Panther fist ("Power to the people!"), but it looked more as if he were showing off something he (and he alone) had just found.

Look what I found. Who knew the Bible was even still around? It's a beautiful and strong book. Very strong! Few know that it was written by Gideon. Great man! Wonderful man! I stayed in one of his hotels once. Incredible!!

The Bible, the president said when asked, was not his *family* Bible. It was just *a* Bible.

Many revere the Bible. Some actually read it.

Enslaved black people read it. They knew the Exodus story and told it to their children, over and over again.

Old Pharaoh used all the force at his disposal to dominate the slaves. But you can keep a lid on a boiling pot for only so long. Tranquility is not peace. And peace without justice is not peace. The mighty shall be brought down. And the downtrodden shall be lifted up. That's what the Good Book says! So the Lord troubled the waters and the lid blew off.

On second thought, maybe the president was just giddy with pride having discovered an explosive device someone had slipped into the Oval Office.

I MYSELF FOUND IT. LOSERS!

If you have a Bible, better hide it now!

RACISM IS SIN

June 14, 2020

This past Sunday I stood with 500 people under a bright sun at the rally for Social Justice in Charles Town. I didn't expect a fiery sermon to kick it off. But that's what happened. The preacher led a call and response.

God is great!

ALL THE TIME

All the time!

GOD IS GREAT

The crowd cheered. I cringed.

Maybe I think too much, but I can't get certain things out of my head. The Crusades. The Black Death. Auschwitz. My Lai. The Killing Fields. Biafra. Rwanda. Lynching trees.

Are you sure God is great? All the time?

I've known this preacher for a long time. We're friends. I know he knows all I know about horrific evils. Still, he's counting on God to pull us through.

The preacher touted the bloody crucifixion of God's only begotten son as the cure for sin. And that triggered a chant.

Racism!

SIN

Sexism!

SIN

Homophobia!

SIN

Xenophobia!

SIN

Racism!

SIN

Jesus died for our sins!

The crowd cheered. I cringed.

Maybe I think too much, but I don't see the crucifixion that way. I don't believe in magic. I think remorse, repentance, reform, and redirecting public funds toward reparations and revamping policing are cures for racism.

I know the preacher knows that too. But he's also counting on Jesus to pull us through.

I thought he was done, but then—as an afterthought—the preacher scolded hypocritical white Christians. (A mask can't hide everything!)

How can you claim to love God (whom you haven't seen) when you fail to love your neighbor (whom you have seen)?

That, he told us, is in the Bible!

The crowd cheered. I cringed.

Maybe I think too much, but there's a lot in the Bible that's downright abhorrent. (Damn homosexuals. Slay the wicked. Wives, submit to your husbands. Slaves, obey your masters!)

That's your moral authority? The Bible?

The sermon ended. Speeches followed. And then we knelt for 8 minutes and 46 seconds to honor the life of George Floyd.

I put my right knee on the brick sidewalk. It hurt. It got worse, minute by minute by minute.

A black man, just in front of me, was sobbing, trembling, sweating. Strangers laced arms around him. Someone handed him a bottle of water and mopped his brow.

Maybe I think too much, but I thought I saw the face of Jesus. Just in front of me.

FOR MOTHERS
(On Father's Day)
June 21, 2020

Today is Father's Day. And as if I that's not enough to crow about, this is my 50th blog post. Each deserves a salute.

But I'll set those aside because a bear waddled through our yard just after midnight last Sunday night. And that just doesn't happen every day. Father's Day and blog milestones come around every year. Bears don't.

The last sighting of a bear in our neck of the woods was 10 years ago. So a bear visit is rare.

We seldom get unexpected visitors out our way—only the occasional Jehovah's Witnesses offering to save us (or else!), or shady characters offering to pave our driveway (or else!). We take *The Watch Tower* pamphlet, or the shady character's business card and politely refer them to our neighbors, completely ignoring the Golden Rule.

Most of the homes along our rural road have signs posted that say, "Protected by ADT" or some other phantom guardian. Not that the bear knows or cares. Bears can't read. But if they could, I'm sure a BEWARE OF DOG sign wouldn't deter them one bit either. *(I'll eat the garbage first and then finish the dog off for dessert.)*

Our dog sleeps inside at night, but when a deer or raccoon or skunk occasionally tiptoes through the yard, Lucy barks her head off. Even a turtle crossing the drive might set her off. Dogs hear things we don't.

A bear merrily plundered our trash cans, tore down two bird feeders, and left harrowing claw marks on a nearby tree. Lucy barked not a word.

Dogs know when to hunker down. My wife doesn't.

She jumped out of bed, grabbed a flashlight, and went out to see what the ruckus was. She's a mother. Ever since our first child lay in a crib, she's slept lightly, both eyes closed, both ears open.

I'm a father. (Here we go!) I sleep like a log. I don't hear babies snuffling or bears snorting.

Thank God for mothers, or else we'd all be dead.

It's not that I'm entirely useless. I keep a baseball bat by the bed in case a bear (or Jehovah's Witness) ever gets into the house.

Said bear is still on the prowl. Neighbors have photos.

Today is Father's Day. My grandsons will be here. I should go out and beat the bushes.

It's OK, Dad. Go take a nap. Mom's got this.

BORN INNOCENT
(What happened?)
June 28, 2020

I was not born a racist. I was not born a misogynist. I was not born a homophobe. I was born innocent.

But I became a racist, a misogynist, and a homophobe.

And a nice guy.

I never denied blacks, women, or gays a mortgage. I never denied blacks, women, or gays a promotion. I never denied blacks, women, or gays a seat on the bus.

I couldn't have even if I'd wanted to. I don't have that kind of power.

But I do have another kind of power.

I attended an integrated high school. I was president of the high school Interact Club, an organization founded by Rotary in 1962. At that time, Rotary was an all-male domain.

My female classmates were not included, never invited. That's just the way it was. And it was wrong.

I never complained, never protested.

Our club had 60 members. The three black members were never nominated for office, never considered. That's just the way it was. And it was wrong.

I never complained, never protested.

My classmates told fag jokes, nigger jokes, and dumb blonde jokes. I laughed.

I never would have kicked, punched, or slapped a black, gay, or female classmate. I was a nice guy. Still, I didn't complain or protest while blacks, girls, and gays were belittled.

I didn't hate any of them. I just didn't love them enough.

I didn't love them enough to walk in their shoes, to feel and see the world as they did. I didn't love them enough to make the world as safe and as good for them as it was for me.

I once was blind. But now I see.

A friend recently asked me: *How can "they" call me a racist when I hold no hatred against any of "them"?*

I told him what I tell myself: *Racism isn't about hating. It's about not loving enough, not loving enough to make the world as safe and as good for others as it is for me. It's not about hatred. It's about indifference. And from that soil, malignant behaviors, policies, and structures arise.*

We are born innocent. And then the learning begins. We learn how to see the world. And we learn how to close our eyes.

And if that's the case, we can learn how to open our eyes and see what we've been missing.

BORN ON THE 5TH OF JULY
July 5, 2020

I was born on the 5th of July. It's an unremarkable date.

It's like January 2 or February 15 or March 18 (if you're Irish) or May 2 (if you're a Druid or a Communist) or May 7 (if you're Mexican) or December 26 (if you're a Christian). It's your birthday, but it's a day late.

A day sooner and people would say: *WOW! A Christmas baby. You and Jesus. Cool.* Or, *WOW! A Cinco da Mayo baby. Bet you like Corona.* (Only when it's in a bottle, thank you.)

I was born on the 5th of July. The day is unremarkable, but the year isn't. I was born in 1947. (OK, boomer!)

Oh, shut up. Don't give me that OK boomer crap. Without my generation you wouldn't be wearing blue jeans to church, writing your own wedding vows, listening to rock 'n' roll in elevators, taking selfies, or saying "dude." We changed the world, dude. No disrespect to the "greatest generation," but they won one war. Big deal! We boomers gave you Pac-Man, Big Macs, and the Bee Gees. Disco, baby. Next time you see one of us, stand up and salute.

But I digress.

I'm retired. I'm in lockdown. I have time. So I Googled "Famous July 5 Births." I won't keep you in suspense. I wasn't among the search results despite all that I've accomplished, for heaven's sake!!

The list I found runs chronologically from 1321 to 1996. (Somebody needs to update that list!)

The first name was "Joan of the Tower," born on July 5, 1321, in the London Tower. She was of royal lineage and so was betrothed at age 7 to David, age 4, son of Robert the Bruce. They married in 1328. David became King of Scotland and Joan became Queen consort. I'll admit, that's fame.

The last entry on the list was Dolly the sheep, the first mammal cloned from an adult somatic cell. Dolly was born July 5, 1996, in Scotland, and named after Dolly Parton. (I won't explain. You can Google that.)

I thought at least one famous person would have been born every year on July 5. That's not the case. The list omitted many years. But only one omission bothered me.

The list jumps from 1946 (Gerard 't Hooft, Dutch physicist) to 1948 (Julie Nixon Eisenhower.)

There's no name by 1947. I've got one. (OK, boomer!)

HAPPINESS
July 12, 2020

My birthday, last Sunday, was nearly a most unhappy one. I started the day on the edge of despair.

My wife's dearly beloved cat went missing the night before. (I like the cat alright. She's nice. She allows me to sleep next to my wife as long as I don't get too close.)

I've watched Meeka develop from an adorable little kitten into something resembling a snooty teenager. Still, I'm quite fond of her. I wish her no harm.

I assured my wife that Meeka would return. After all, she'd stayed out all night once before. But, of course, that was before a bear cub began prowling our woods.

A cat that goes missing on the Fourth of July, I told my wife, is probably declaring her independence. (Paula didn't think that was funny!)

A statue of St. Francis stands in our flower garden watching over all creatures, great and small. So I knew Meeka would be at the back door in the morning.

I slept well and got up before sunrise, eager to confirm my faith.

Meeka was not at the door. She was not there at 6, 7, or 8 a.m. My wife would awaken soon. I foresaw weeping and gnashing of teeth.

I summoned our black lab, Lucy, to join me in searching for "little sister." We tromped about the woods. Lucy sniffed and sniffed.

I called out like the good shepherd searching for the lost sheep. In that Bible story, there were 99 other sheep back home. This story has only one cat in it. One cat. Period.

In the Bible story there's a happy ending. The shepherd finds the lost sheep, lifts it in his arms, and carries it back home. The heavens rejoice.

We were not in the Bible. We were in the woods. Deep, dense woods.

We tromped farther. Time passed. Hope faded. We slouched back to the house. Defeated.

And there she was.

Meeka was sitting in the middle of the backyard, near the statue of St. Francis, nonchalantly licking her paws.

My heart nearly burst.

I skipped up the stairs like an evangelist bearing the good news of salvation. My wife beamed. The heavens rejoiced.

I've often thought that happiness is overrated. It's fickle, chancy, circumstantial, like happenstance.

Joy is better. It runs deeper. It's unflappable.

But on the morning of July 5, 2020, happiness was joy.

The cat came back.

GRAVEN IMAGES
July 19, 2020

We have a statue of St. Francis in our flower garden. So far no one has attempted to topple it.

Even the bear cub—during its midnight rampage a few weeks ago—left St. Francis standing despite toppling two trashcans on one side of the statue and tearing down two bird feeders on the other side.

What can I say? *Everybody loves St. Francis.* The same can't be said of Robert E. Lee, Columbus, or the Golden Calf.

I hadn't given statues much thought, but when I did I couldn't help thinking of the Golden Calf and Moses' rampage against it. He tore it down.

Moses hadn't been gone but a few days when his people blatantly violated the Second Commandment. *Make no graven images.*

Which makes you wonder what our compatriots in the Bible Belt were thinking when they installed hundreds of graven images. Don't they read the Bible?

(When my evangelical friends tell me that the Bible is the Word of God, I have to ask them: *Really? Have you ever read it?*)

Anyway, all these pious people who want to post the Ten Commandments in courthouses and public places had better read the blessed list first.

Sabbath observance alone would eliminate Sunday football and NASCAR. The prohibition against killing would eliminate war and capital punishment. The adultery clause—punishable by stoning to death—would eliminate many judges, lawmakers, and at least one president.

Our Bible Belt compatriots revere the Second Amendment. The Second Commandment, not so much.

Moses might have been the first iconoclast, but he wasn't the last.

Sixteenth-century Protestants demolished thousands of Catholic icons and statues in the name of righteousness. It wasn't the statues themselves that were odious. It was the values they represented and enshrined.

These days moral absolutism drives a lot of people. I'm all for righteous causes, but I find self-righteous people unbearable. (*God save me from your people!*)

Even our hungry, prowling bear cub was discriminating. You don't have to destroy everything just because you're hungry.

Beware what you idolize. Especially your own truth.

Knowledge increases. Values evolve. Circumstances change.

This is no time to revere icons of genocide, treason and White supremacy. Now is the time to repent and make amends.

We need a statue to humility.

Until then, I say, tear 'em all down. Except two.

St. Francis in my garden.

And Mr. Bojangles in Richmond.

AT THE BEACH
July 26, 2020

As you read this I'm at the beach in Avon, North Carolina. Depending on when you read this, I could be doing any of the following:

Brewing coffee and unloading the dishwasher before anyone else in the house gets up (my job)

Sipping coffee on the deck, watching the sun rise over the Atlantic

Pedaling down highway 12 through a morning breeze—ocean on one side, sound on the other—toward the Buxton lighthouse

Smearing on sunscreen, strolling 100 yards over a couple dunes to the beach

Standing ankle deep in the lapping surf, trying to get up the courage to plunge in

Bodysurfing and/or regaining my balance (and wits) after a vicious face plant into the pebbly seafloor

Rubbing my face and neck, considering a safer water activity

Floating like a log on my back as only old men know how, thinking I'm cool, knowing I'm not

Sitting on a beach chair reading *The Brothers Karamazov* on my Kindle, smoldering, turning pink

Wiggling into flip-flops, plodding over the dunes back to the house

Rinsing sand off under an outdoor shower, drying off, pulling on a dry bathing suit

Watching CNN "breaking news" during lunch, wishing I hadn't ("there's nothing new under the sun")

Taking a nap, recovering from my morning activities

Working the *New York Times* crossword puzzle

Smearing on sunscreen, strolling over the dunes back to the beach for afternoon activities (see above)

Plodding back over the dunes, back to the house

Putting on evening wear (slippers, shorts, and T-shirt)

Lounging on the deck, listening to a playlist, snapping open salted peanuts, quaffing cold beers, awaiting the call for dinner, snapping, quaffing, snapping, quaffing

Eating with family around a large table, reveling in merriment

Rinsing dishes, loading dishwasher, sorting recyclables (my other job)

Lounging on the deck, chit-chatting with my wife, and/or children, and/or grandchildren, and/or pesky seagulls, and/or drinking until dusk

Sitting on the sofa with my grandchildren who crave my attention and advice (not)

Sitting on the sofa with my grandchildren watching a Disney movie

Hugging them before they go traipsing grudgingly downstairs to their bedroom and I go lumbering gladly off to mine

Sleeping, knowing tomorrow will be another grueling day

Some people say, "Things can't make you happy."

That's not true. (See above.)

At the beach.
Wish you were here.
But wherever you are, may you be happy.
Randy

ODE TO EVE
August 9, 2020

On the way to the beach last week we passed Kitty Hawk. And that got me thinking of Eve. (It had been a long drive.)

Think what you will about Eve, but she launched her children into space. NASA, China, and the United Arab Emirates each launched a spacecraft toward the Red Planet last month.

Thanks to Eve our reach will always exceed our grasp.

I know the Church portrays Eve as a villain, plunging humankind into sin and darkness. But I don't see it that way at all, nor do most Jews who first told the tale of the forbidden fruit.

Eat that fruit (of knowledge) and you will die, warned the divine potter who had molded Adam and Eve. *I'm divine and you will never be.*

We'll, see about that, muttered Eve.

A serpent cheered her on. *You won't die. You'll come alive! You'll become something the rest of us can't be. Your children will be the wildcards of creation!*

I see Eve as a hero, defying "God" and (we might say) patriarchy and all restrictions on her aspirations. This tale from the Great Ancestors portrays humanity's ascent, not its descent.

Of course, it's a folktale—not history or anthropology. It's not factual. But it is meaningful.

It articulates human capabilities (and vulnerabilities). Yes, we go awry—badly. But that comes with an evolved (and evolving) brain as complex and baffling as the entire cosmos.

Unlike the other animals, amazingly intelligent, sophisticated, and adaptive as they may be, the human animal distinctly manifests limitless curiosity, ingenuity, and inventiveness—divine-like powers to create (and destroy!). We don't need the Bible to tell us that. We can see it for ourselves.

We traveled to North Carolina in a gasoline-powered automobile, a machine invented by two bicycle mechanics, brothers Charles and Frank Duryea, who showed it off on September 21, 1893, in Springfield, Massachusetts. Top speed: 7.5 mph.

It took us six hours to reach Kitty Hawk from Shepherdstown.

The Wright brothers took a train from Dayton through West Virginia to Hampton Roads, a steamer to Norfolk, a train to Elizabeth City, and a schooner to Kitty Hawk, toting all their gear on and off each conveyance for seven days to launch a 605-pound, motor-powered plane 852 feet for 59 seconds. December 17, 1903.

One hundred seventeen years later three spacecraft are bound for Mars.

Owed to Eve.

(Stand down, brothers.)

ODE TO THE BIKE
August 16, 2020

I write these things at a certain time on a certain day and that certain time this week was threatened by an old friend who wanted to go on a bike ride during my blog writing hours. I know I mustn't give in to temptation or my work will suffer. It might not get done.

But he is a good friend.

And I do like my bike.

I notice it leaning against the stair rail. It's a marvel of human ingenuity.

First, you need to invent the wheel.

Wings, fins, webbed feet, and lenses are found in nature. People noticed them and fabricated imitations.

Wheels are not found in nature—unless you count logs, certain stones, or a dung beetle's prized turd ball, which rolls like a wheel. It's not likely a caveman saw that and thought "wheel." The turd ball evoked possibilities, but "wheel" wasn't one.

The first wheel was fabricated about 6,000 years ago. It was around for millennia before someone thought to affix an axle so two wheels could roll in the same direction. And thus, the cart.

Millennia went by.

And then in 1817 a certain Baron Karl von Drais paired two wheels, front and back, and connected them with a wooden frame, ridiculed as "the dandy horse." Soon after came pedals, chains, gears, pneumatic tires, aluminum, and the Tour de France.

In the late 19th century bicycling clubs formed in Europe and America. Those elite clubs lobbied for smooth, paved roads. Later, automobiles would hog those roads built for bikes.

The bicycle is the most efficient human-powered means of transportation. There are twice as many bikes as cars.

But it's more than a marvelous machine.

Experiments done in Uganda, Tanzania, and Sri Lanka show that a bicycle increases a poor family's household income as much as 35%.

For women, the "noiseless steed" brought liberation and bloomers. Susan B. Anthony called it the "freedom machine."

"I think the bike has done more to emancipate woman than any one thing in the world," she said. "I rejoice every time I see a woman ride by. It gives her a feeling of self-reliance and independence. The moment she takes her seat, away she goes, the picture of untrammeled womanhood."

A bike goes on forever. Friends don't.

Work can be postponed. Living can't.

I said yes to my friend.

I took my seat. Away I went. Untrammeled.

FOR SUCH A TIME AS THIS
August 23, 2020

For if you remain silent at this time, relief and deliverance for your people will arise from another place, but you and your family will perish. And who knows but that you have come to your position for such a time as this? (The Book of Esther)

I watched the Democratic national convention Monday night. I heard the prophet's voice: *Come on up for the rising. Come on up, lay your hands in mine.* (Bruce Springsteen, *The Rising*)

Can't see nothin' in front of me
Can't see nothin' coming up behind
I make my way through this darkness

Hell has broken lose. But heaven is before us *like a catfish dancin' on the end of the line.* Within reach. But it just might get away.

America is on fire. The towers of freedom and justice have been struck. Not from above. But from below. A cabal of torch-wielding swamp creatures have struck the pillars of our nation.

It's late. But not too late.

Still, many don't see the fire. Or pretend not to. Some put on blinders. Some turn on HBO. Some fiddle. Some play golf.

But others have seen the fire, heard the bell, and answered the call to save our nation before it's consumed.

These are the times that try men's souls. The summer soldier and the sunshine patriot will, in this crisis, shrink from the service of their country; but he that stands by it now, deserves the love and thanks of man and woman. Tyranny, like hell, is not easily conquered; yet we have this consolation with us, that the harder the conflict, the more glorious the triumph. What we obtain too cheap, we esteem too lightly: it is dearness only that gives everything its value. (Thomas Paine, *The Crisis*, December 23, 1776)

We can't see the light. We make our way through the darkness.

We don't know the end. We walk by faith.

We take another's hand. We hang on to hope.

There comes a time when one must take a position that is neither safe, nor politic, nor popular, but one must take it because conscience says it is right. (Martin Luther King Jr., *A Testament of Hope*)

Ours is not the musket.

Ours is not the firehose.

Ours is the ballot.

SYMPATHY FOR THE DEVIL
August 30, 2020

Please allow me to introduce myself
I'm a man of wealth and taste
I've been around for a long, long year
Stole many a man's soul to waste
("Sympathy for the Devil," The Rolling Stones)

I'm a registered Democrat. My father and his father were too.

My father worked as a brakeman on the P&LE railroad. His father was a Pennsylvania coalminer. My father's uncle was a union organizer.

My father's father died young, soon after a coalmining mishap, leaving seven children and their mother behind. The company offered no compensation. *Sorry, it wasn't our fault.*

His uncle was blackballed. *Sorry, no work for you today.*

My father was a union man. Later he became disenchanted by the corruption. Still, he told me: *A bad union is better than no union at all. The capitalists always exploit the working man.*

My father saw the world in black and white. Good and evil. Workers and owners. Protestants and Catholics. He grew up in a mixed coalmining village. German Lutherans were honorable. Irish Catholics were not.

My parents were born-again fundamentalists. By age 5 I knew the world was divided into Baptists and Papists. By age 10, I knew the world was divided into Democrats and Republicans.

I once asked my father about the two parties. He told me: *Democrats look out for the working man; Republicans look out for the businessman.*

I know now it's not that black and white. Still, I remain an unapologetic social democrat. I'm loyal to my tribe. (I'm also an Orioles' fan.)

I watched the Democratic convention. I liked it.

I thought it was so convincing that the Republicans would throw in the towel and forfeit the race. After all, they could have no answer to the Democrats' arguments.

I was wrong.

I watched (some of) the Republican convention. As it turns out, they have answers.

Good is evil. Evil is good. Fact is fiction. Fiction is fact. Real is fake. Fake is real. White is black. Night is day. Up is down. Heads is tails. Hate is love. Lies are truth.

Yes, it's terribly confusing.

But what's puzzlin' you is the nature of my game. Pleased to meet you. Can you guess my name?

I know, I know. I know that's unkind. I know it's unfair. And I know it's not helpful.

But sometimes I just can't help myself.

(Must be the devil in me!)

* * *

Listen to "Sympathy for the Devil" by the Rolling Stones on YouTube

SHIP OF FOOLS
September 6, 2020

I've been reading Plato's *The Republic* for the second time. The first time was in college 50 years ago. I was a philosophy major. It was required reading.

So was *The Brothers Karamazov*. I recently reread that classic of love, betrayal, money, murder, and insanity. Fun. And just like that, August flew by.

Reading a book without the pressure of writing a paper or taking an exam is so much more enjoyable. Like running without weights. I figure two or three more Russian novels and this pandemic will be over (or I'll be insane).

In college, I took Greek for four years, so I read portions of *The Republic* in its original language. I wrote a paper. I passed the exam. I don't know how. The book is obtuse in any language.

Still, I committed to plowing through it again (all 10 books). I also regularly bang my head against the *New York Times* Sunday crossword puzzle. I've heard that reading obtuse books and working crossword puzzles can prevent dementia. (We'll see.)

I took up *The Republic*, in part, because I wanted a diversion from the "ship of fools." I needed a breather. Nothing like visiting the rational philosophical dialogues of fourth century BCE Greece to get away from this plague of anxiety.

I would breathe fresh Hellenic air. I would revel in wisdom. I would chew lotus. I would forget. Ah, antiquity.

It didn't work out so well.

Unfortunately, parts of *The Republic* are clear as day. For example, Plato compares the state to a ship and asks: *What would happen if we entrusted the navigation of a ship to a rich man—who knew nothing about piloting—just because he was rich?*

Gulp.

And then later, in regard to a state ruled by a tyrant adored by the gullible masses, he says: *When the tyrant has disposed of foreign enemies by conquest or treaty, and there is nothing to fear from them, then he is always stirring up some war at home, in order that the people may require a strong leader.*

I closed the book and pushed it aside.

I'm now rereading *Mad* magazines.

A LAMENT FOR EVANGELICALS
September 13, 2020

Some of my best friends are evangelicals.

I attended Wheaton College—*A Christian liberal arts college 25 miles west of Chicago in a tree-shaded suburb.* I made friends.

Wheaton is the Harvard of the evangelical world. (Or so we were told.) We read all the famous dead white guys. None were evangelical.

We read Sophocles, Plato, Aristotle, Aquinas, Descartes, Hume, Milton, Schopenhauer, Dostoevsky, Kierkegaard, Ibsen, Sartre, Hegel, Darwin, Marx, Freud, Bertrand Russell, and, on the side, *Mad* magazine.

After Wheaton I attended Fuller Seminary in Pasadena, the premier school of theology for evangelicals. I made more friends.

My evangelical friends were Democrats.

We stood against the Vietnam War. We stood for civil rights, for a woman's right to choose, for the United Farmworkers, for nuclear disarmament, for McGovern. Many of those friends went on to mobilize against apartheid, for same-sex marriage, for the Paris Agreement, for Black Lives Matter.

We knew our evangelical heritage was morally flawed. But we channeled the best of it.

We respected the revivalists of the early 18th century who "awakened" pride and dignity in poor American colonists. We admired evangelicals at the forefront of the abolitionist movement, women's suffrage, unionization of workers, and the elimination of child labor.

For 200 years evangelicals had been a force for good, even though (I would guess) 20% or so were despicable. That's not so bad. I suspect the same percentage applies to Rotarians, Episcopalians, Jews, Muslims, Buddhists, Amish, atheists, and the Mickey Mouse Club.

Evangelicals had been a force for good.

And then along came the Moral Majority.

Jerry Falwell became the face of evangelicalism, a voice touting racism, homophobia, and Christian nationalism. Evangelicals suddenly sniffed political power and sold their souls to get it.

In college I read Goethe's *Faust*. Faust sold his soul to the Devil. The transaction was fiction. Or so I thought. I now know it isn't. I've seen it happen.

Evangelicals compose 25% of the population; 80% of them voted for this president.

I left evangelicalism 40 or so years ago. I still respect its social justice heritage but not its Bible-thumping or its White Republican Jesus.

I cannot forgive evangelicals their betrayal. I cannot excuse their apostasy, hypocrisy, duplicity, and stupidity.

I look at evangelicals today and I don't see the faces of my friends anywhere.

I would weep if I weren't so damn mad!

BEELINE MARCH
September 20, 2020

Today I will stand with fellow citizens at a "Rally for Racial and Economic Justice." We will stand on the site where the "Beeline March" began 245 years ago, a site now known as Morgan's Grove Park. It's in Jefferson County just outside Shepherdstown, West Virginia. In 1775 it was in the colony of Virginia.

I wouldn't call it sacred ground, although Alexander Boteler did. Boteler's father, Henry, built a house (Fountain Rock) on that site in 1834.

On July 19, 1864, a detachment of the Union army under Captain Franklin Martindale burned it to the ground in retaliation for General Jubal A. Early's burning of the Maryland governor's house—all part of the war to end slavery.

Burning property as a form of justice!

Imagine that!

If you're rallying for justice, Morgan's Grove is a pretty good place to stand.

In July of 1775, 98 Virginia riflemen assembled there under the leadership of Captain Hugh Stephenson at the request of General George Washington by way of the Continental Congress. They made a "beeline" to Cambridge, Massachusetts—600 miles in 25 days—to join the battle for freedom.

The revolution was imperiled. More bodies were needed. They answered the call to liberate their country from British tyranny. They turned the tide.

This Sunday we are rallying a different kind of army—voters—who will make a beeline to the ballot box or mail box to liberate our nation from a different kind of tyrannical oppression. More bodies (and votes) are needed to turn the tide decisively.

The Rev. Ernest Lyles asked me to offer the invocation at the rally. I agreed even though I don't do traditional invocations anymore. Invocations "invoke" God's presence. I don't think that's necessary.

For whatever God is, God is always present. No need to invoke what's already here. As the ancient Greek poet put it: *In God we live and move and have our being.*

I'm not even sure what God is. You can name it what you will. I just let the mystery be. But I'm guessing it's love.

God is love. God is present. God is awake.

I'm not sure about the rest of us.

So I think provocation is needed more than invocation. I'd like to "provoke" dozing citizens to wake up.

Don't sleep through this revolution or you might wake up in a country you don't recognize anymore.

HOUSE ON FIRE
September 27, 2020

Just when I thought the winds of change were blowing in the right direction, Ruth Bader Ginsburg has to up and die. Jeez. Here comes the whirlwind.

How many more freaky things can happen?

I wouldn't rule out anything.

Jesus returns, raptures Jews; stupefied evangelicals are left behind.

Martians land, deliver a COVID-19 vaccine to the White House.

Jared Kushner wins the Nobel Peace Prize.

(GULP. GAG. VOMIT.)

(Sorry.)

As I was saying, I had been feeling positive and hopeful.

I saw three Biden-Harris signs in Sharpsburg, that proud hamlet of the Confederacy. Last election, not a one for Hillary. So that's a good omen.

West Virginia is sprouting Biden-Harris signs. Last election, I saw only a few for Hillary. Another good omen.

Our own Biden-Harris sign posted along our secluded road was stolen. We got another and donated another $10 to the Democratic Party.

(If you're the thief and reading this, please know that we will do so again and again and again. But then, maybe you're a Democrat without a penny to spare and wanted a sign of your own. God bless you. Keep taking them. Every sign counts.)

Still, I'm not counting on signs to sway voters. As far as I can tell, few are left to sway.

Polarization has driven us into two camps with only a few stragglers wavering between, as if one camp were no different from the other. If you're flipping a coin at this point, you should have your eyes, ears, and nose examined.

There is no moral equivalency.

Maybe in times past. Not now.

The choice isn't between the lesser of two evils. The choice is between good and evil (allowing for a 5% margin of error).

Once upon a time, truth mattered. Once upon a time, integrity mattered. Once upon a time, civility mattered. Once upon a time, decency mattered. Once upon a time, kindness mattered. Once upon a time, the law mattered. Once upon a time, the Constitution mattered.

They still do. Please, don't forsake them.

One side has set the house on fire. But it's a big house.

Yes, much has been lost already. But much is still standing, and fires can be quenched—*as long as the fire truck arrives before it's too late.*

And that's why this election matters more than ever.

STILL WATERS
October 4, 2020

> *When despair for the world grows in me*
> *and I wake in the night at the least sound*
> *in fear of what my life and my children's lives may be,*
> *I go and lie down where the wood drake rests*
> *in his beauty on the water,*
> *and the great heron feeds.*
> *I come into the peace of wild things*
> *who do not tax their lives with forethought of grief.*
> *I come into the presence of still water.*
>
> Wendell Berry, *The Peace of Wild Things*

* * *

I read the news. I study the polls. I remember.

My stomach's in knots.

I opened an old book and betook myself to Walden, far from the madding crowd, far from death counts, burning forests, and the dismal swamp. I sat in the doorway with an old friend and gazed upon the mist hovering above the pond.

He had no radio, no television, no newspaper.

The sun rose.

A woodchuck waddled by.

A loon wailed.

I spoke of my worries, anxieties, and rage.

He pointed to his garden. He pointed to the birds. He pointed to the trees. These were his neighbors, his companions. He knew each by name.

We walked around the pond and into the woods. Leaves and twigs crunched beneath our feet. Squirrels scampered. Butterflies fluttered. Flies and other insects darted hither and yon. A breeze brushed by.

Time stopped. The past, the future, the present were one. We walked through four seasons and back to his doorway.

We sat in silence.

Can a man by taking thought add one inch to his stature? he asked out of the blue.

No, I replied.

Do the birds of the air or the flowers of the field worry themselves about tomorrow?

No, I replied.

Who sees the sparrow fall?

He stood, walked inside, and shut the cabin door.

I returned home.

I knelt by our fish pond. I listened to the birds. I gazed at the woods. I watched leaves falling, the season turning.

The sun set. The moon rose. An owl hooted. I fell asleep.

The election ended. The president conceded.

Civility returned. Racism receded. Democracy revived.

The mountains rejoiced.

The hills skipped like lambs.

The trees of the forest sang.

The lion lay down with the lamb.

And a little child led them beside still waters.

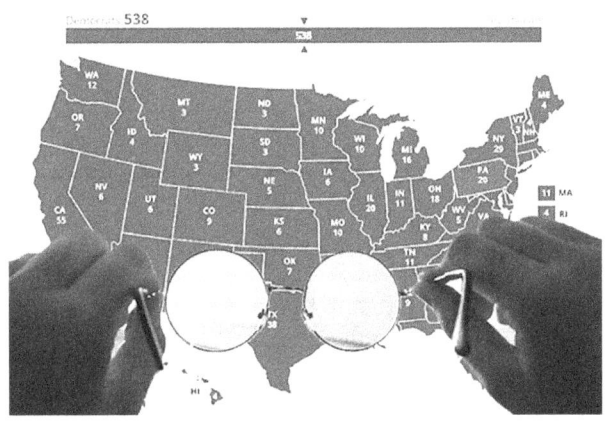

POSITIVE THINKING
October 11, 2020

The president tested positive for COVID.

I gloated.

I told myself not to, but I couldn't stop. I was actually on the verge of rejoicing. (*That's not nice!* I told myself.)

So I tried to conjure sympathy.

I told myself he's president of the United States. I told myself he's a fellow human being. I told myself he has wives and children.

Still, I felt no sympathy. I just can't console an unrepentant abuser. That would enable him even more.

And yet it seemed the whole world was praying for him.

I wasn't.

I revere nature. I believe in natural laws. I don't believe in a god who saves people from stupidity.

I don't know for sure, but I'm guessing the president initially saw his test result as a compliment, as some sort of praise.

Of course my test was positive. I'm a positive guy. I was weaned on Norman Vincent Peale's The Power of Positive Thinking. *It's the only way I think.*

Think happy thoughts and you will be happy. Say you're a winner and you will win. Believe a virus will disappear and it will disappear.

The power of positive thinking has never failed me.

Against all odds I was elected president. Despite numerous bankruptcies, a fraudulent university scheme, stiffing contract workers, boasting of adultery and denigrating Mexicans, Muslims, disabled people, women, and American war heroes, I was elected president. I even got 3 million fewer votes than my opponent and still won.

THINK POSITIVE AND GOOD THINGS WILL HAPPEN.

And then someone explained to him that a "positive test" in this case was not a good thing and that he could die.

NO PRESIDENT HAS EVER FACED A CHALLENGE AS GREAT AS THIS. NO PRESIDENT HAS VOLUNTARILY TAKEN ON THE SUFFERING OF HIS PEOPLE. NO PRESIDENT HAS BEEN MORE LIKE JESUS.

And just like that, the president realized this could (AND WOULD) turn out for his benefit because everything always did. EVERYTHING.

The whole world thinks I'm on my deathbed. But I will rise on the third day. I will dominate death. The world will rejoice. Hymns will be sung. Behold, the Dominator!

I stopped gloating and started thinking positive. STRONGLY!

The votes will resound.

The Dominator will deflate.

America will mend.

America will smile.

America will shine from sea to shining sea again.

I'm thinking positive. I'm hopeful.

But I ain't feelin' it.

Not (quite) yet!

MIRACLE ON PATRICK STREET
October 18, 2020

Paula and I drove to Frederick this past Sunday to have lunch with two friends we hadn't seen for what seems ages. On the ride over we counted political signs along the roads and highways. It's what we do these days.

We saw more signs for our side than the other.

It's too soon to be giddy, but we did feel a twinge of optimism. The tide is rising, but we don't say that out loud lest we tempt the fates or arouse the demons lurking in the pesky electoral college!

We arrived at JoJo's Tap House.

"Inside or out?" the receptionist asked.

The forecast was for rain. We glanced at the sky, sniffed the wind, and checked our weather apps. We requested a sidewalk table and took our seats—and chances—along Patrick Street under an oak tree.

As it turns out, this is fall. Hello!

For two hours a hail of acorns would pummel us. Every five minutes or so one would ricochet off the table. One plunked my head. (I should have worn my bicycle helmet.)

One bounced off the sidewalk right into our friend's glass of water. I asked the server if that meant we'd won a stuffed animal. (No, it did not.)

Our order arrived. We raised our glasses. We broke bread. We praised the crab dip. We relished our sandwiches and hand-cut fries, not to mention Frederick's finest ale.

Acorns kept pelting us. We laughed and raised another glass.

We talked of former days, of treasured memories, of adventures and mishaps unknown till now. We caught up on our children and grandchildren. We spoke of sorrow, of friends now gone.

We talked on through the hailstorm never once speaking "The Name."

It can be done.

The server delivered the check. We requested a photo of our happy reunion. She gladly took our smartphones in turn. We smiled. Smiled again. And again. We thanked her. She smiled. I left a handsome tip.

Let's do this again, we said. *Let's do.*

We donned our masks, held our breath, and hugged each other—signs of friendship on Patrick Street in historic downtown Frederick. (Kisses would have to wait for another time.)

We drove back to Shepherdstown with a bundle of fresh memories and hearts full of joy. We didn't count the signs along the way.

For the moment we were counting our blessings.

THE GOD WHO SMITES
October 25, 2020

My longtime friend is a secular Jew, which makes him, I think, a humanist. He hasn't renounced his Judaic heritage, but he takes it with a grain of salt.

Hard not to, what with the "talking snake," Abraham's near sacrifice of his son Isaac, the plagues of Egypt, blood in the rivers, the frogs, the boils, the slaughter of the firstborns, manna from heaven, the whole "Promised Land" bit, not to mention the "Chosen People" thing. That's a lot to swallow!

Over the years I came to share my friend's aversion to religion. Under his influence—and a host of thoughtful skeptics such as Baruch Spinoza, Thomas Paine, and Bertrand Russell—I gradually discarded theism (trust in a supernatural god) in favor of humanism.

Humanism gives prominence to nature, natural law, and science. It expects human ingenuity to solve problems. Humanists aren't superstitious. Humanists don't expect any god to save us.

My friend now believes in such a god.

A few weeks ago when a close associate of the president tested positive, my friend fell to his knees and asked the god of his ancestors to smite the president with the virus, and if his ancestral god would do that, my friend would gladly make a sacrifice.

The next day the president tested positive.

My friend immediately redialed Jehovah. My friend thanked Jehovah and then explained that he had only daughters, so sacrificing his firstborn son wasn't possible. Instead, he would give up drinking beer until after "The Election."

I know how much my friend likes (loves!) beer. I thought he was joking. But he insisted it was true, and he certainly didn't want to go back on his word with a god who smites people.

I told him that this sort of superstition (*Let's try something here. Kill a chicken and see if it rains!*) is what gave rise to religion in the first place. He shrugged it off. He's keeping his promise to Jehovah.

I saw him last week. He has definitely lost weight.

Well, as it turns out, the whole *positive test–Walter Reed Hospital–Il Duce balcony appearance thing* turned the electorate against the incumbent. My friend's prayer did it!

If Biden wins, I will mold a statue of my pious friend, place it next to St. Francis in my flower garden, and every November 3rd salute it with a pint of beer.

GOODBYE, MR. PRESIDENT
November 1, 2020

Goodbye, Mr. President. I did not like you. I did not like you a little. I did not like you one bit.

But now that you're leaving I will say, I did admire a few things about you.

You're a winner. But then, *winning* is a relative term. You can win the battle and lose the war. You can win the world and lose your soul.

I admired your effort. You did the best you could. But *best* is a relative term. Your best was not good enough for this country.

I admired your sincerity. You mean what you say and say what you mean. But then, *sincerity* is a relative term.

Charlie Brown lost every game he pitched and in exasperation asked his girl pal Lucy: *How can I lose when I'm so sincere?*

Charlie was sincere. But he was also a lousy pitcher.

I admired your authenticity. You speak from your heart. But *heart* is a relative term. It matters what's in the heart.

When the Golden Calf is your idol, it turns your heart to stone. You trample over people, laws, and virtues to grasp the Golden Ring. I'm sorry your father fed you lies. (I do not admire him.)

Finally, I admired your magnetic charisma. You sure put a spell on your base. Other than the followers of Mussolini, Jim Jones, and the Philadelphia Eagles, I can't think of any group more loyal than yours. But *loyalty* is a relative term.

Lemmings are loyal.

I don't know, but I can guess that at least one lemming plunging to death over a cliff behind its revered leader thought: *I should have been more skeptical.*

Mr. President, you've lost. But it's not as if all is lost. You can still be saved.

According to the Apostles' Creed, *Christ descended into hell to save sinners.* But then, *hell* is a relative term.

It's more likely you'll go to a penitentiary. But cheer up. Think positive. It's a great place to do penance. (*Penitent-iary.* Get it?)

Another good thing about going to prison is: *evangelicals have a fabulous prison ministry.* They'll be there with you every day. (Be sure to take your Bible.)

And with any luck, your boy pal Jerry Falwell Jr. will be your cellmate.

Talk about winning!

You just can't lose!

WHAT, ME WORRY?
November 8, 2020

I worried Tuesday night. I worried the next day. I worried all week. But I set worry aside to bury my cousin yesterday.

My cousin Dolores died last month in Jacksonville, Florida. It was an agonizing death. Her kidneys and liver gave out. She was in and out of comas. Still, she faced death valiantly. She was a devout Christian and a devout Republican.

She voted for the president.

We hadn't seen each other for years. And then out of the blue I heard the news.

I missed most of her life. I wish I had known her better. We would have disagreed on much, but we would have gotten along. We're family.

Yesterday we interred her ashes at the Sylvan Heights Cemetery in Uniontown, Pennsylvania, next to her father, my uncle Joe, and her two brothers, my cousins David and Donny. Her father and my father were brothers.

I have ten cousins on my father's side. As children we frolicked together every summer. The days were long. And then long gone. We grew apart. Distant.

Now only five of us remain. We've grown old. Saturday we stood together under the shadow of death.

Family.

We don't choose our family. Families are given. We might not like each other or see eye to eye, but we find a way to get along—somehow, if not easily.

We don't choose our fellow citizens either. Compatriots come with the territory. We might not like each other, but we must get along.

The funeral ended.

And then THE NEWS broke!

We now have a chance to come together. I could worry that we won't.

But, alas, worrying gets us nowhere.

I Worried
by Mary Oliver

I worried a lot. Will the garden grow, will the rivers
flow in the right direction, will the earth turn
as it was taught, and if not how shall
I correct it?
Was I right, was I wrong, will I be forgiven,
can I do better?
Will I ever be able to sing, even the sparrows
can do it and I am, well,
hopeless.
Is my eyesight fading or am I just imagining it,
am I going to get rheumatism,
lockjaw, dementia?
Finally I saw that worrying had come to nothing.
And gave it up. And took my old body
and went out into the morning,
and sang.

OUR SIDE WON
November 15, 2020

Seventy-three million Americans (10 million more than last time!) voted for the president even after I plainly stated on this site weeks ago: *For once the choice is not between greater and lesser evils. This time it's black and white. Good versus evil.*

Seventy-three million!

I'm baffled.

How could they? Are they blind or demented?

Who let such people in our country? Where was the wall when we needed one? Where's a basic intelligence poll test when we need one?

Please answer this question before I give you a ballot: Was John Brown sane or insane, saint or villain, liberator or terrorist?

And the answer is ... ?

Therein lies the problem. Who's to say? Who would be right?

Every morning before I take on the news, I take up a book—biographies usually. Recently I read about the lives of three African Americans who migrated out of the lynching Jim Crow South in the early 20th century in *The Warmth of Other Suns,* by Isabel Wilkerson.

Currently, I'm reading *John Brown, Abolitionist,* by David Reynolds.

As it turns out, half the nation saw John Brown one way, the other half another way, just as our nation is divided in its perception of the president. Messiah or Mussolini?

No, the president is not John Brown. Brown conceded defeat graciously. Even Henry Wise, governor of Virginia, considered Brown a "true gentleman" (but still sent him to the gallows!).

There are, however, similarities between Brown and the president.

Each dominated national news for a long spell. Each forced the nation into polarized camps. Each has been deemed a tyrant and/or insane.

Pottawatomie John Brown of "Bleeding Kansas" led a murderous attack on Harpers Ferry, and still his Northern base supported him. Not all, but many. Thoreau, Emerson, and Henry Wadsworth Longfellow did.

Earlier, William Lloyd Garrison, a pacifist abolitionist, rebuked the extremely devout, Bible-waving, Calvinistic Brown for defying Christ's commandment in the New Testament: *Love your enemies.* Brown replied: *I'm an Old Testament Christian.*

Abraham Lincoln also denounced Brown's violence. Lincoln said persuasion would work better. And then Lincoln did what Brown did at Harpers Ferry. He invaded the South with armed forces.

The nation was bitterly divided. Each side touted different values. Each saw the other as enemy. Each claimed God was on its side.

I would never claim God is on our side.

I'm just glad our side is right.

THANKSGIVING
November 22, 2020

Today before sunrise I woke up in a sturdy bed, under cozy covers, and on a firm mattress. None of which I had made.

I got out of bed.

I flipped on the light switch by the bathroom mirror and squeezed toothpaste onto a brush. None of which I had made.

I brushed my teeth.

I reached for pants, shirt, socks, and shoes. None of which I had made.

I dressed.

I walked down steps across a floor into the kitchen and turned on the coffee machine. None of which I had made. Nor had I grown, cultivated, harvested, packaged, shipped, or shelved the coffee.

I sipped my coffee.

I placed a bowl and a spoon on the kitchen counter. None of which I had made.

I filled my bowl with grains, nuts, seeds, spices, and fruit. I did not grow, cultivate, harvest, package, ship, or shelve any of those ingredients.

I ate breakfast.

I put on my jacket, picked up my coffee, opened the back door, let the cat out, and stood on the deck. I heard birds chirp. I saw shadowy trees sway and morning stars wane. I watched the sun rise over South Mountain and shine through the woods wherein stood a cautious deer. None of which I had made.

I turned away.

I had a blog to write.

I went to my office, sat down at my desk, turned on my computer and some classical music. I stared at a blank page. I scratched my head for a subject. Nothing.

Well, what about Thanksgiving?

What about it? It's contrived, isn't it? It's like my mother often said: *if you're not mindful of me on other days, don't call me on Mother's Day.* (She could be sassy!)

If you're not mindful of me!

Suddenly I saw what I had missed at every turn this morning. I had gotten out of bed, but I had not awakened.

I will never meet all those—in heaven or on earth—who made my life so rich this morning. But If I could, I would say, "Thank you."

Meister Eckhart said*: If the only prayer you ever say in your entire life is "thank you," it will be enough.*

I suppose if we were mindful all day every day, that's the only prayer we'd have time for.

The world is full of grace.

It's hard to miss it.

But we do.

A DAY OF MOURNING
November 29, 2020

Our national Day of Thanksgiving has come and gone. And so has the national Day of Mourning. Both were commemorated this past Thursday. The one by millions. The other by a handful of Native Americans at Plymouth, Massachusetts.

Most Americans celebrate the Pilgrims landing in 1620. Native Americans do not. Most Americans buy the myth of Pilgrim philanthropy toward the Wampanoag. Native Americans do not.

Since 1970 the United American Indians of New England have commemorated a National Day of Mourning. It's a day to honor Native ancestors and Native peoples' struggle to survive. It's a day of remembrance as well as protest against racism and oppression that Native Americans still experience. It's preceded by a day of fasting.

I get it. Life is not always jolly.

There is a time to dance and a time to mourn.

Still, I can celebrate Thanksgiving without swallowing the Pilgrim myth, just as many celebrate Christmas without swallowing the Virgin Birth, the serenading angels, or the Magi's astrology. We wink at the myth and embrace the spirit of the day.

We give thanks. We exchange gifts. We let the myth have its day.

But myths are not facts.

I cherish many myths—Santa Claus, the Easter bunny, the rising phoenix—but I cherish the truth more.

The Pilgrims and their successors undertook the genocide of millions of Native peoples, the theft of Native lands, and a relentless assault on Native cultures.

We have many holidays for merrymaking. But we don't have a holiday for mourning, a time to pause and remember our transgressions.

The Jewish people do. On Yom Kippur they remember their sins, their failures at love and justice. It's a day of fasting. It's solemn but not sad. Mercy greets the repentant.

When we remember our transgressions, confess, and make amends, we find redemption. We walk in the light. When we forget or deny our transgressions, we walk in darkness.

We can be thankful any day. But Thanksgiving concentrates the mind on gratitude.

We can be remorseful any day. But a day of remembrance would concentrate our minds on contrition.

On such a day we would acknowledge the ways we have wounded ourselves and others, including Mother Earth and her creatures. We would fast. We would confess. We would weep. We would resolve to make reparations.

We need a national Day of Remembrance.

A humble nation becomes a better nation.

A LONG DARK WINTER
December 6, 2020

LIFT EVERY VOICE AND SING
Stony the road we trod
Bitter the chastening rod
Felt in the days when hope unborn had died
Yet with a steady beat
Have not our weary feet
Come to the place for which our fathers sighed?
We have come over a way that with tears has been watered
We have come, treading our path through the blood of the slaughtered
Out from the gloomy past
'Til now we stand at last
Where the white gleam of our bright star is cast

James Weldon Johnson (1871-1938)

I hear talk of "a long, dark winter." And I hear talk of "light at the end of the tunnel."

If you're an optimist, that light is sunshine.

If you're a pessimist, that light is a long, long, long way off.

If you're a realist (or cynic), that light could be a train's headlamp.

Well, it could be.

Hope has been crushed before.

In August 1619, English settlers of the Virginia colony purchased 20 Africans. And thus began a long, long, long dark winter for Africans in this country. Over the next 250 years thousands of Africans arrived in chains and shackles to be bought and sold.

To balance Southern representation in Congress, the US Constitution counted a slave as "three-fifths a person." The Fugitive Slave Act of 1850 declared enslaved people "property." Runaways would be returned to their owners like runaway mules. The Dred Scott decision of 1857 denied citizenship to anyone of African ancestry.

The long, dark winter persisted.

And then on January 1, 1863, Abraham Lincoln issued the Emancipation Proclamation. Frederick Douglass and other abolitionists rejoiced. They saw light at the end of the tunnel. Finally!

Free at last! Thank God we are free at last.

But hope was soon crushed.

Promises were broken.

Reconstruction collapsed.

The federal government refused to enforce civil and voting rights established in the 14th and 15th Amendments. White supremacy strode on, lynching thousands, torching homes and churches, suppressing black votes. Jim Crow ruled the South. Blacks were incarcerated by the thousands.

The long, dark winter persisted.

Persists.

Well, at least one long, dark winter will soon be over. A vaccine is coming our way at warp speed!

It's amazing what we can do when we want to. It only takes focus, will, ingenuity, and a lot of money.

COVID is not all that ails our nation.

NIGHT
December 13, 2020

Today is the third Sunday of Advent. The third candle stands for joy.

Tonight I will light that candle with a trembling hand and a broken heart. My young friend died last Sunday night by his own hand.

There's no joy in that. There's no joy for his mother. There's no joy for his friends.

Still, we will light the candle. We must. We must face the darkness. We must lift up our hearts.

Somehow.

I met him when he was just a wee babe. His adoptive father and mother beamed, more radiant than the sun. Their newborn son was golden.

I baptized him. I watched him grow. I watched him blossom.

He was the darling of our church.

He squirmed on the pew Sunday after Sunday between his proud mother and father. He looked up to them. His heroes.

His father sang in the choir. The boy watched, proud of his daddy.

And then out of the blue, a crash. His father died. No warning. No goodbyes.

My young friend was five years old. I stood beside him at his father's grave.

There's no joy in that.

My young friend made his way. Somehow. He sang in the choir. Like his father. He charmed the ladies of the church. Like his father.

He graduated. He found a job. He fell in love. The future was wide open.

And then this.

Darkness.

In the beginning darkness covered the face of the deep. And God said, Let there be light. And there was light. And God separated the light from the darkness. God called the light "Day" and the darkness "Night."

God did not eliminate darkness from the world. God named it. And sometimes that's all we can do. We name the darkness and let it be. For out of the darkness life arises. Time and time again.

Somehow.

Eventually.

In the meantime, we light the candles of faith, hope, and joy. And next Sunday, the candle of peace.

Advent is a season of darkness. It's a time to sit in solidarity with all who sit in darkness. We face it together. We long for the sun's return.

When my friend was just a child, he stood with me in the chancel of the church and lit the candles on the Advent wreath. One by one.

Beyond the dark night of his soul I believe my young friend saw a light.

VACCINE
December 20, 2020

Today is the fourth Sunday of Advent. Advent is a time of waiting, expectantly, hopefully, for the arrival of someone or something. Many Christians await the Second Coming of Jesus but settle for Santa.

Advent comes around every year and is quickly swallowed by Christmas. But this year is different. This year Advent hit the jackpot.

THE VACCINE IS HERE!

The Advent of the Vaccine is the greatest news since the Birth of Jesus!

Do not be afraid. Behold, I bring you good tidings of great joy for all people. For unto you this day in the city of David—and ten thousand other sites—a vaccine is borne.

Shepherds tending their flocks by night hoist their masks and shout: *Glory to God in the highest!*

And then I heard the angels exclaim, ere they flew out of sight, *Merry Christmas, Joseph!*

Joseph?! What about Mary?! What about Jesus?!

And then I saw the angels' meaning. Joseph can be Joe. Of course!

MERRY CHRISTMAS, JOE BIDEN.

And, of course, that too is an advent to celebrate.

The advent of normality.

The advent of stability.

The advent of adults, diplomats, scientists, wise men and women arriving at the White House bearing facts, understanding, and goodwill.

JOY TO THE WORLD!

Tonight I will gladly light the candles of faith, hope, joy, and peace.

I will celebrate the advent of a new president. I will celebrate the men and women who counted the votes. I will celebrate the advent of the vaccine. I will celebrate the men and women who brought it to us.

Faith, hope, joy, and peace. Indeed!

But Advent is not over—there's still four days to Christmas. Tonight I will remember those who walk in darkness. I will remember 310,000 COVID deaths in our country and the millions who grieve them.

Alas, this year many—so, so many—face a blue Christmas. Nothing can console. Twinkling lights can't. Carols can't. Candles can't. A vaccine can't. (It's too late for the dead.) Tonight and for many nights to come, millions will trudge through the godforsaken valley of the shadow of death.

So tonight we light the candles of faith, hope, joy, and peace for those who can't. It's not much. But it's something.

There's no vaccine for sorrow. There's only companionship.

Be not afraid. You are not alone. Friends and neighbors walk beside you.

And where love is, God is.

STAR OF BETHLEHEM
January 3, 2021

Epiphany, celebrated on January 6, commemorates the adoration of Jesus by magi from the East. They had observed an astrological sign pointing to the birth of a Jewish king.

They set off following a certain star west to Jerusalem. The star patiently waited (twiddling its thumbs) for them to finish consulting with King Herod before leading them south to Bethlehem.

There they knelt before the child.

Some say the star of Bethlehem was the conjunction of Jupiter and Saturn. Some say it was a comet, a supernova, or a double occultation of Jupiter by the moon.

Oh, stop!

The star of Bethlehem is poetry. It's Jewish poetry echoing the prophet Isaiah's song that had been in the Jewish Top Ten for 500 years.

> Arise, shine; for your light has come,
> the glory of the Lord has risen upon you.
> Nations shall come to your light,
> kings to the brightness of your dawn.
> Lift up your eyes and look around;
> they gather together, they come to you;
> A multitude of camels shall cover you.
> They shall bring gold and frankincense.
> Violence shall no more be heard in your land,
> nor devastation or destruction within your borders.

That's a dream from a battered and beaten people, not unlike our own.

Imagine all the people sharing all the world.

We don't need astronomers to verify the Bethlehem star any more than we need them to verify the star that appeared at the birth of Emperor Augustus.

We don't need gynecologists to verify the virgin birth of Jesus any more than we need them to verify the virgin birth of Romulus and Remus.

And when a poet says: *My love is a rose*, we don't need a botanist.

It's poetry. It's devotional language. We use it all the time. *My granddaughter is the most beautiful child in the world!* We don't need beauty pageant judges.

The beautiful child of Bethlehem would become not a king but a servant, one who knelt before others to wash their feet. This child of Judaism would do justice, love kindness, and walk humbly with God.

The world doesn't need a king or messiah. The world needs servants of love.

If you follow the star of Bethlehem today it will lead you to yourself. It will show you that you are a beautiful child of God.

That's an epiphany.

And that will bring you to your knees.

BAPTISM OF JESUS SUNDAY
January 10, 2021

On the second day of this new year I walked the battlegrounds of Antietam. My grandsons merrily dashed up and down rolling hills and gleefully splashed in mud puddles, despite their mother's earnest pleas.

That day I heard other pleas from other mothers, many other mothers.

I've walked those grounds many times. But this time was different. I saw and heard things I hadn't seen or heard before.

(Not all epiphanies are sunny.)

I recently rewatched Ken Burns's "The Civil War" PBS series. It's replete with heart breaking letters to and from brave but terrified young men.

Mother, tonight I sleep in the mud. I hear artillery in the distance. I don't know if I'll ever see you again.

I saw piles and piles of dead young men. There. There. And there. They had dashed across hills and fields into a barrage of fire. Nearly all were baptized Christians. Each side said God was on its side.

And God was.

On both sides.

Women on both sides—Clara Barton in the North and Cornelia McDonald in the South and 10,000 nameless others—stanched bloody wounds, soothed fevered brows, moistened parched lips, and consoled the dying. Nearly all were baptized Christians.

Today is the Baptism of Jesus Sunday. It's a minor holiday on the liturgical calendar. There are no gift exchanges. There are no candy baskets. No red helium balloons as on Pentecost.

As told in the gospel, the baptism of Jesus was spectacular. The heaven's opened, a dove descended, a voice spoke. "You are my beloved son. Today I have begotten you."

(Maybe there could be doves on the Baptism of Jesus Sunday. Lots of doves.)

Jesus would heal the sick, feed the hungry, soothe the tormented, welcome outcasts, and love his enemies even if it killed it him. It did. Love didn't win that day.

He was crucified, dead, and buried.

Jesus's body lay a-moldering in the ground, but the truth went marching on, right onto the battlefield of Antietam and so many other godforsaken places.

We don't need investigators to verify the resurrection of Jesus any more than we need them to verify the resurrection of Osiris.

Mother, tonight I sleep in the mud. I hear artillery in the distance. I don't know if I'll ever see you again.

And then a nurse knelt beside him in the mud and wiped his brow.

God was on both sides.

STORMING THE CAPITOL
January 17, 2021

Think how stupid the average American is and then consider half are stupider than that. George Carlin

* * *

A raging mob stormed the Capitol on Wednesday, January 6. Honestly, I've felt like doing that myself numerous times over the past 50 years. Alas, over these past four years I've even felt like storming the White House just about every other day. I've felt like punching a few faces and wringing a few necks in both places.

I know about strong feelings. I have many. But I don't act on them. At least not all of them.

I'd like to think I'm not stupid. I try to reason things out a bit before acting.

Anger is a powerful force. It's a reaction to injustice, real or perceived. Nothing wrong with that. We can't help our reaction. It's normal, it's healthy, it's human.

Reactions are spontaneous. Responses are not. We can manage them.

Despite my strong feelings of anger and disgust, I would never invade the Capitol—*unless the entire West Virginia legislature somehow suddenly occupied both houses.*

January 6 was the Day of Epiphany. Epiphany commemorates the arrival of wise men from the East bearing gifts to Jesus in Bethlehem. As far as I can tell there wasn't a single wise person in that giddy mob on Wednesday.

(Note to insurgents: If you manage to lure a Trojan horse with a hollow wooden head into the capital of the United States and lurk in its bulging belly for four years, you'd better have a plan when you roar out of the horse's ass—something other than milling around, posing on parapets, commandeering chairs, defecating in hallways, giggling up your sleeve, and waving "Jesus Saves" signs.)

(Note to Jesus: *Please save us from your people!*)

History is peppered with attempted coups and insurrections. But none was as dumb as this one.

At least the British assault in 1814 had battalions. This one had buffoons.

On second thought, maybe stupidity isn't all bad.

It may have saved our republic.

Let's bring back Betsy DeVos.

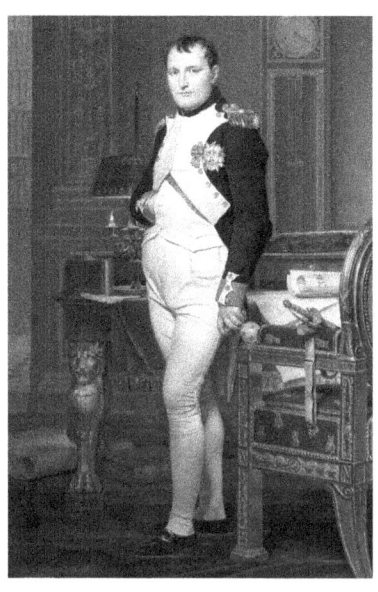

NAPOLEON EXILED

January 24, 2021

We will be back in some form
Donald Trump, January 20

* * *

Trump is not Napoleon. The United States is not France. The 19th century is not the 21st.

And yet.

Napoleon was born a Corsican, under the umbrella of Genoa. He was loyal to Italy until he saw greater opportunities with the French. He switched parties.

Corsica is not Manhattan. Paris is not Washington.

And yet.

The Revolutionary government in France was unpopular. The masses were angry. Napoleon betook himself to Paris.

Napoleon was charismatic. He hoodwinked the electorate. He squelched the assembly of legislators. He was proclaimed First Consul. In December 1804, he crowned himself emperor—with the pope's blessing.

The pope is not Jerry Falwell Jr.

And yet.

In 1813 Napoleon straggled back to Paris from his catastrophic military defeat in Russia, claiming victory. Britain, Austria, and Prussia were poised to invade France. And just like that, fact trumped fiction. Yielding to public pressure—and with the guillotine glistening—Napoleon abdicated.

The European allies sent him packing to Elba, a small island off the western coast of Italy. To humor him, the British granted him a pension, a sizable staff, and a title: Sovereign of Elba.

Napoleon bided his time.

Louis XVIII now ruled France. The reign of the Bourbons was restored. But it lacked luster (and liberality). The people grumbled. The grumble reached Elba.

Napoleon slipped off the island and back to France. He wended his way to Paris. Village after village cheered him on. The savior of the nation had returned. The army defected from Louis XVIII one battalion after another.

In Paris Napoleon received a hero's welcome. He reclaimed his crown, rebuilt the army, and set off gallantly to Belgium to crush the forces poised to remove him again. He met his Waterloo. He hobbled back to Paris, claiming victory again.

But the French had wised up. They'd seen enough. The defrocked (and corpulent) emperor was exiled to St. Helena. He never came back.

Impeachment is not exile. Mar-a-Lago is not St. Helena.

It doesn't matter.

Biden is president. Kamala Harris is vice president. Democracy is restored.

The long, cold, lonely winter is over.

On Wednesday America found what it had lost—sheer joy. We saw smiles returning to faces—from sea to shining sea.

Lady Gaga sang our national anthem.

America stood up.

The sun shone.

Our flag waved.

I wept.

WELCOME TO EARTH, BABY
January 31, 2021

The insurrection came. The impeachment came. The inauguration came.

And then along came Magnolia. Reluctantly.

(Who can blame her?!)

My young friend became a mother last Sunday night. She delivered on her promise. ("I'm gonna have a baby!") She produced an 8 pound, 6 ounce girl. Greer Magnolia. A star was born.

("Sugar Magnolia!")

It wasn't easy. No birth is. But some are harder than others. This one was really, really, really hard. The promised one had a mind of her own.

She ignored the due date memo.

("You will be arriving at platform B on January 14.")

She bided her time, sheltering in place.

("It's safe in here! It's scary out there!")

She defied the tug of nature.

("Slow down. You move too fast. Gotta make the morning last!")

She dug in her heels against induced labor.

("I hear you knocking but you can't come in!")

Facebook posted hourly briefings. Hundreds sat on pins and needles, chewing on fingernails in a virtual waiting room.

But she couldn't hold out forever, twiddling her thumbs backstage. That's not the way it works. The stage is lit. The curtain is up. We can't hold our breath forever. You've gotta come up soon for air, baby. We want to hear your song.

And just like that (easy for me to say), there she was skimming through rays of violet, wading through a drop of dew, gulping the air of this wild and wonderful world.

I've baptized a few babies in my time (including Magnolia's mother). If I could hold them all in my arms again, I'd whisper in their ears the words of Kurt Vonnegut.

Hello, baby. Welcome to Earth. It's hot in the summer and cold in the winter. It's round and wet and crowded. On the outside, baby, you've got a hundred years here. There's only one rule that I know of, baby—"God damn it, you've got to be kind."

That's a good rule for babies. That's a good rule for children. That's a good rule for parents. That's a good rule for everybody.

The insurrection came. The impeachment came. The inauguration came.

And then along came Magnolia blooming in the sunshine.

("Come on, honey. Come along with me.")

Hope is abornin' in our nation. Birth is never easy. Sometimes it's really, really, really hard.

But the stage is lit.

The curtain is up.

* * *

Listen to "Sugar Magnolia" by the Grateful Dead on YouTube

SUPER BOWL 2021
(Revisited)
February 7, 2021

I attended tonight's Super Bowl last year—in a dream. I shared that dream in my blog post on Mother's Day (May 9, 2020). See below. Nothing in that dream will happen tonight. But something nearly as incredible will. America's first rock-star poet, Amanda Gorman, will read a poem at the Super Bowl tonight. POETRY. AT THE SUPER BOWL. TONIGHT. I'm now thinking my dream isn't too far off.

* * *

I dreamed.

I sat in a stadium, larger than the Coliseum. Super Bowl 2021.

I saw the flags of every nation encircling the rim of the stadium. At one end flew the Olympic flag; at the other, the flag of the United Nations.

The stands were packed with people from all nations, festooned in native garb. Vendors hawked cuisine from every continent.

A gong rang. Drums rolled. Trumpets blew.

I looked for the presentation of the colors by each branch of the military.

Instead, another kind of battalion strode onto the field. A company of nurses. A company of doctors. A company of EMTs. A company of scientists. A company of custodians. A company of bus drivers. A company of police. A company of grocery clerks. A company of school teachers. From every nation.

Spectators leapt to their feet, waving and cheering.

I looked for the military flyover.

Instead, three cargo planes lumbered overhead: one bore the UN insignia, another the Red Cross, another the Red Crescent.

A choir of children assembled.

We all sang in our native tongues: *We Are the World.* (*We are the children.*)

Silence.

No one ordered it. It just happened. It went on and on. (No one was keeping time.)

Two people hugged. Two more and two more. A wave began, waves of hugs rippled across the field and through the stands.

And then the battalion began walking off. The stadium rocked with applause.

The teams trotted onto the field. Not two. Two hundred.

No helmets. No shoulder pads. No cleats.

Instead, silly hats, funky pants, soft shoes.

Ten health workers strode onto the field for the coin toss. Dr. Anthony Fauci flipped a coin. (It turned into a dove.)

The players took their places. A whistle blew. Bean bags flew.

Partisans roared.

The International Corn Hole Games were on.

Bean bags soared, skidded, and thumped all afternoon.

Players squinted, sweated, swore, and switched sides all afternoon.

Partisans roared all afternoon.

Points were tallied all afternoon. (No one kept score.)

The games ended.

No injuries. No concussions. No losers.

Every team won.

The bars were jammed that night.

The next day the president addressed the nation. "The budgets for the Pentagon and the NIH will be swapped," she said. "I'm a mother. The time has come. The world will have a brighter day! All its children will be safe."

I woke up.

* * *

Listen to "We Are The World" by Michael Jackson on YouTube

VALENTINE'S DAY
(Ugh!)
February 14, 2021

Today is Valentine's Day. I'm not a big fan.

As a prepubescent boy I got a lot of candy hearts from many a prepubescent girl who wanted to "be mine" or "kiss me." I thought kissing a girl would be icky, but still I chewed their candy, got cavities, went to the dentist, and had a shrieking drill plunged into my rotten tooth.

(Love hurts.)

The origin of Valentine's Day is murky. In the third century CE Roman Emperor Claudius II executed two men named Valentine in two different years, both (by freaky coincidence) on February 14.

(The Romans didn't fool around with wimpy things like impeachment.)

The Roman Catholic church canonized both Valentines as martyrs, established February 14 as St. Valentine's Day, and bought stock in Hallmark, Cadbury, and FTD.

(I can't swear to the stock purchase bit, but it wouldn't surprise me.)

There's more.

From February 13 to 15, the Romans celebrated the feast of Lupercalia to venerate and invigorate sexuality and fertility. Men sacrificed goats and dogs and then romped naked through the streets whipping women with thongs cut from the hides of the slain animals.

(Eat your heart out, QAnon!)

In the fifth century Pope Gelasius combined Lupercalia and St. Valentine's Day hoping to squelch the pagan fertility revelries. Men complained, but dogs and goats sang *te deum laudamus* at the top of their lungs.

(I can't swear to the *te deum* bit, but it wouldn't surprise me.)

Shakespeare romanticized Valentine's Day.

My lips, two blushing pilgrims, ready stand / To smooth that rough touch with a tender kiss.

(If only those candy hearts had borne such poetry, I might have dared a kiss!)

And thus a tradition was born. In 1913 Hallmark Cards of Kansas City, Missouri, cheerfully adopted it. Valentine's Day became a $20 billion bonanza.

I'm not a fan. I'm not a fan of bonbons, teddy bears, or heart-imprinted underpants.

But I am a fan of love songs.

I Just Called to Say I Love You. Something. I Will Always Love You. Wonderful Tonight. Love Me Tender. Annie's Song. Ain't No Mountain High Enough. At Last. Endless Love.

And that's just a start.

It's hard to pick a favorite. But I do have one: "In Spite of Ourselves," by John Prine.

It's a quirky song but then so is true love.

HAPPY VALENTINE'S DAY.

In spite of this blog!

*　*　*

Listen to "In Spite of Ourselves" by John Prine & Iris DeMent on YouTube

GIVING UP LENT
February 21, 2021

Today is the First Sunday in Lent. I'm not giving up anything. I'm not taking on anything. I'm happy with the way I am. It took a lot of years and a lot of effort to reach this point.

I'm not smug. I'm content.

I don't eat chocolate much. I don't drink much. I don't eat meat much. I don't chew tobacco.

I don't curse much. I don't judge others much. I don't hate the president anymore. I don't hold grudges.

I love my neighbor as myself. I don't covet my neighbor's wife. I don't make graven images.

I do unto others as I would have them do unto me. I love my enemies and bless those who curse me. I don't give alms, but I do donate to nonprofits and Democratic candidates. I believe in equality and justice for all.

I render to Caesar the things that belong to Caesar and to God the things that belong to God. I pay my taxes. I remove box turtles from the road.

I don't turn stones into bread. I haven't sold my soul to the devil in exchange for power, glory, and dominion. I don't leap off high cliffs expecting God to save me. I don't believe in that kind of God. I believe in facts not fantasy, reason not religion. I believe in love.

I consider the lilies of the field and the birds of the air and don't fret about tomorrow. I honor my parents and don't abuse my children. I bring my pets in when it's freezing cold.

I don't carouse much. I rise early. I do yoga. I eat oats, nuts, and berries for breakfast. I take a nap after lunch. I bike three days a week and walk in the woods the other days. I cut and split my own firewood.

I read for an hour or so every morning. I work on my blog or my new book for a few hours. I shun Facebook. I answer emails promptly. I don't tweet.

I observe the Sabbath.

It may be Lent but I don't need to give up anything or take on anything. I'm happy with the way I am.

I'm not smug. I'm content.

I'm not vain. I don't toot my own horn.

Yes, I lie.

But not much.

NOT LONG TO LIVE
March 7, 2021

This past Monday, I said yes. I should have said no. And now I regret it.

I haven't felt this sad since we had our sweet Rita euthanized two years ago. Her legs and hips were shot. We nursed her along as long as we could.

It was the right thing to do. But still it hurt. She gazed into our eyes a long while. And then her eyelids slowly closed.

I live in the woods. We built our house among countless trees. We put down roots. We became neighbors with the trees.

Some are majestic. Some runty. Some are vibrant. Some sickly. I like them all. But as it turns out, one tree in particular had won my deep affection.

It stands within a rock break. My grandsons and I occasionally sit in its shade eating sandwiches. It's a special tree in a special place.

Our woods includes a dozen ash trees. We can count on them dying, along with another eight billion in North America. The emerald ash borer is working its way across the continent. There's no cure. No vaccine. Ash trees are falling left and right, day and night.

Power companies mark them for removal.

On Monday the chainsaws arrived to remove marked trees. My favorite tree wasn't marked.

What about this one, asked the man with the chainsaw. *It's not got long to live. As long as I'm here, shall I take it down?*

I said yes and returned to the house.

(A friend once told me: *Make reversible decisions quickly; irreversible ones slowly.*)

I heard the roar of the saw. I heard the groaning of the tree. I heard the thud.

It's not got long to live.

But not long can be a while.

I now wish I could sit under its shade with my grandsons one more summer, whiling away our time together. I should have said no.

TREES
by Alfred Joyce Kilmer

I think that I shall never see
A poem lovely as a tree.

A tree whose hungry mouth is prest
Against the earth's sweet flowing breast;

A tree that looks at God all day,
And lifts her leafy arms to pray;

A tree that may in Summer wear
A nest of robins in her hair;

Upon whose bosom snow has lain;
Who intimately lives with rain.

Poems are made by fools like me,
But only God can make a tree.

WIZENED BEAUTY

March 14, 2021

Last Sunday I shared my grief over the felling of an ash tree. As it turns out, the emerald ash borer is slowly killing them all.

I know the feeling. Age is boring into my bones. I'm sagging.

(Gravity sucks!)

All my friends are getting old. One just turned 70. Another 90. When I was 30, people that age looked awfully old.

Someone once told me that anyone 20 years older than you looks old. At 20, 40 looks old. At 40, 60 looks old. At 60…well, you get the idea.

I'm 73. Anyone still alive doesn't look old to me.

Peers I see regularly still look young. We're like trains moving in the same direction on parallel tracks. Both are moving, but it doesn't feel like it.

That has a certain comfort to it until you go to a class reunion.

A few years ago I walked into my 50th high school reunion and saw a classmate I hadn't seen for years. *Oh my God, what happened to you?* I thought. (Don't say it!) I bit my tongue. But the tongue is a rascally muscle. I blurted it out.

What do you mean what happened to me? retorted my old friend, staring at my wizened countenance.

Fortunately (or unfortunately), I've had a lot of practice with blunders like that. Many a time I've blurted out something that should not have been said. So over the years my tongue's become like Jack—nimble and quick.

You look more beautiful than ever! I hastily replied.

And then I noticed that was actually true.

Beauty ages like fine wine.

Minutes later I was called to the microphone to give the invocation. When you're the only minister in a class of 300, you're stuck with that dubious honor.

(I didn't know Randy became a minister! And to think I thought he was really cool back then!)

I dislike proforma prayers. I had none to offer. But I did have a blessing for all to recite with me, plus a freshly conceived idea.

Love before us, love behind, love under our feet.
Love within us, love over us, let all around us be love.

And then I asked everyone to turn to the person next to them and say: *Oh my God, what happened to you? You've never looked more beautiful!*

A ripple of hugs went round the room.

And that was really cool.

ARE WE ALONE?

March 21, 2021

*The universe is a pretty big place. If it's just us,
seems like an awful waste of space.* —Carl Sagan

* * *

My friend believes extraterrestrial life is out there. I'm skeptical but I'm not a denier. I'm agnostic.

Could be.

Might be.

Probably is.

Probably is, given the population of our Milky Way—300 billion stars and at least that many planets—not to mention a trillion galaxies beyond this one, each with a trillion stars and a trillion planets. There are a zillion possibilities.

My friend believes extraterrestrial life is out there.

Avil Loeb does too. Loeb, the longest-serving chair of Harvard's department of astronomy, thinks there's hard evidence for his belief.

On October 19, 2017, astronomers at the University of Hawaii spotted a bright speck tumbling away from Earth and eerily veering away from the sun. The object was named 'Oumuamua and classified as an interstellar asteroid.

Loeb disagreed with that classification. To him it did not look or act like an asteroid or a comet. He surmised it was a "light sail" launched by a technologically sophisticated civilization somewhere, somehow, some time ago. He makes his case in *Extraterrestrial: The First Sign of Intelligent Life Beyond Earth*.

"It would be arrogant to think we are alone," he told a reporter.

Loeb became a media sensation even though most in the scientific community consider his theory kooky. Still, he presses on because that's what real scientists do, he says. (Think Galileo.)

Loeb grew up on a farm in Israel. He read Jean-Paul Sartre and Albert Camus. He dreamed of becoming a philosopher. He joined the army, enrolled in the advanced weapons program, and worked on laser technology. He became a physicist and wrote a doctoral dissertation entitled: "Particle Acceleration to High Energies and Amplification of Coherent Radiation by Electromagnet Interactions in Plasmas." (I haven't read it.)

Loeb discovered a lot. But one question keeps nagging him:

Are we alone?

If we discover other intelligent beings out there, we will be humbled, he thinks.

Which got me thinking.

Aren't there plenty of other reasons to be humble?

Earth is a grain of sand in the cosmic sea. It took 4.5 billion years for humans to stand up on the planet. Millions of other animals arrived long before us. Without bees and trees we'd be dead.

We do not stand alone.

We cannot stand alone.

We are not alone.

EARTH IS OUR GIG

March 28, 2021

When I consider your heavens, the work of your fingers,
the moon and the stars that you have established;
what are humans that you are mindful of them,
mortals that you care for them?
Psalm 8

* * *

Last Sunday I posed the question: "Are we alone?" Is the human animal the only intelligent form of life in the universe?

(We could, of course, debate whether we are "intelligent." But let's set that aside.)

The post prompted many comments. Everyone agreed that thinking we're the only intelligent life form in the universe is naive given the expanse and age of the universe (14.5 billion years and still expanding). In fact, innumerable intelligent beings may have already come and gone.

Still, we keep looking into space and emitting radio waves.

Hello. Anybody out there?

But as one reader put it, other life forms may be nothing like us—carbon based, or physical, or even on our wavelength. So it's like looking for a needle in a haystack without a clue as to what a needle is.

Astrophysicist Avi Loeb, author of *Extraterrestrial Life*, cherishes our planetary home and our species. But he fears we've been too short-sighted given our likely extinction. If a pandemic or a nuclear or climate apocalypse doesn't kill us all, the sun's eventual demise will.

But, alas, all species are programmed to survive!

So Loeb and others are conspiring to disperse synthetic human cells (like dandelion seeds) throughout the universe hoping that one or more will alight on another habitable planet and propagate our species long into the future. "Panspermia" in reverse!

(I'm leery. I see reasons to keep us quarantined.)

Loeb was raised in the Jewish tradition. He learned about Eve's defiant reach for knowledge. (Not even God would stop her!) Loeb also learned the creation story that proclaims human "dominion" over the earth.

But dominion is not domination. Dominion is a responsibility. (A lot of Christians sure misread that one!)

As one reader put it: *Alone or not, Earth is our gig.*

I don't believe God "gave" humans dominion. I believe humans discovered their "divine-like power" to create and destroy, a power no other animal has.

Some take that power as a license to exploit and destroy. Others take it as a responsibility to creatively care for the earth and all that dwell therein.

It's a choice.

We might even say, it's an IQ test.

Michelangelo's *Pietà*, photo by Erik Törner/Flickr

MARY DON'T YOU WEEP

April 4, 2021

Today is the first day of Easter. Easter is a 50-day season. Today is also the last day of Passover. Passover is a seven-day observance. Today is the beginning of one, the end of the other. A rare convergence for two "movable feasts."

(Easter always falls on the first Sunday after the first full moon after the vernal equinox. April 4 this year. Passover always begins on the first full moon after the vernal equinox. March 27 this year.)

Both holidays commemorate deliverance.

Passover celebrates the deliverance of the Hebrew people from bondage in Egypt. Easter celebrates the deliverance of Jesus from death, a crucifixion by the Roman Empire.

Both celebrations claim a historical, factual origin.

Moses parted the Red Sea. The Israelites crossed over safely. Pharaoh's pursuing army drowned.

Jesus was buried. A massive stone covered the mouth of his tomb. Three days later he arose, fully alive, nail marks on his hands and feet.

Many people believe that's exactly what happened—in both cases.

I don't.

I can't.

I believe in natural law. Seas don't part with a wave of a hand. Dead bodies don't rise up.

And yet they do.

My head doesn't get it. But my heart does.

O Mary don't you weep, don't you mourn. Pharaoh's army got drowned. O Mary don't you weep.

Emmet Till is dead.

George Floyd is dead.

O Mary don't you weep, don't you mourn.

Breonna Taylor is dead.

Soon Chung Park is dead.

O Mary don't you weep, don't you mourn.

Martin Luther King is dead.

Gandhi is dead.

Anne Frank is dead.

Michael Collins is dead

John Brown is dead.

Sarah Good is dead.

Joan of Arc is dead.

Jesus is dead.

Moses is dead.

Hate, bigotry, and fear are not.

O Mary don't you weep, don't you mourn. Pharaoh's army got drowned. O Mary don't you weep.

I don't believe in miracles. I believe in hope.

I believe you can take a sad song and make it better.

I believe you can take a tragedy and weave a tapestry.

I believe you can take a fallen tree and make a table.

I believe you can take a broken nation and mend it.

O Mary don't you weep, don't you mourn. Pharaoh's army got drowned. O Mary don't you weep.

I believe in hope.

I believe in good work.

And music that revives the dead.

* * *

Listen to "O Mary Don't You Weep" by Bruce Springsteen with the Sessions Band (Live in Dublin) on YouTube

ABOUT THE AUTHOR

Randall Tremba was born and raised in Youngstown, Ohio. He took a bachelor of arts in philosophy at Wheaton College, Illinois (1969), a master's of divinity at Fuller Theological Seminary, Pasadena, California (1973), and a doctor of ministry at Princeton Seminary (1992). He was installed as minister of the Shepherdstown (WV) Presbyterian Church in July 1976. Forty-one years later he retired. In between, he married Paula, became a parent (Jonah, Nathanael, Amanda) and a grandfather, founded the Rumsey Radio Hour (1990), and co-founded the Shepherdstown *Good News Paper* with Ed Zahniser (May 1979). In June 2017 he published his first book, *Let Love Arise: 40 Short Essays*. (Available at Four Seasons Books, Shepherdstown, WV). And in June 2019 he launched his blog "The Devil's Gift." You can subscribe at www.thedevilsgift.com. Contact the author at randy@thedevilsgift.com.

www.ingramcontent.com/pod-product-compliance
Lightning Source LLC
Chambersburg PA
CBHW051401290426
44108CB00015B/2103